OTTO BENESCH

REMBRANDT

AS A DRAUGHTSMAN

PHAIDON

OTTO BENESCH

REMBRANDT

AS A DRAUGHTSMAN

AN ESSAY

WITH 115 ILLUSTRATIONS

PHAIDON PRESS

MADE IN GREAT BRITAIN
TEXT PRINTED BY HUNT BARNARD & CO · LTD · AYLESBURY · BUCKS
PHOTOGRAVURE PLATES PRINTED BY VANDYCK PRINTERS LTD · BRISTOL
COLOUR PLATES PRINTED BY BALDING & MANSELL LTD · WISBECH

SOME WORDS ON REMBRANDT'S DEVELOPMENT AS A DRAUGHTSMAN

REMBRANDT's drawings form the part of his work to which scientific consideration was given last. Whereas his etchings had already been catalogued in the eighteenth and his paintings at the beginning of the nineteenth century, the drawings were not catalogued until the beginning of our century, in Hofstede de Groot's fundamental work. The master himself never regarded them as objects of financial speculation as we know that he did his prints. Contemporary writers report that Rembrandt, during the time of his economic prosperity, used to increase the commercial value of his prints by buying them up at the highest prices at public sales, a kind of financial speculation which was not unusual among the artists of seventeenth-century Holland. During Rembrandt's life, most of his drawings were carefully kept in the cupboards of his studio, classified in separate portfolios according to subject, as we learn from Rembrandt's inventory taken in the year of his bankruptcy, 1657. Only a few passed out of his possession: into the hands of his friends, if they were leaves of albums; or into the hands of customers, if they were portraits highly finished like etchings or paintings. Most of them remained in use in the studio, or – the smaller and less important ones – passed into the hands of pupils. Rembrandt needed his drawings first of all for his own work.

In the later Middle Ages the common use of a drawing was as an instrument in preparing a composition: as a diagram of a complete conception, or for settling details. A drawing at that time was not regarded as a definite means of artistic expression, nor was it an independent and self-contained work of art. It was either an illustration of a literary text or a scientific note, or it was a note for the execution of a work to be built, painted or modelled. In the beginning of the sixteenth century, artists in the Netherlands and in Germany first made drawing a special manner of artistic expression to be presented only in *this* way and in no other. Many drawings by Lucas van Leyden, Dürer and Altdorfer are works of art in themselves, expressing completely what their authors wanted to say, and not intermediate steps to a higher form of artistic expression. These drawings were esteemed and collected by art lovers and amateurs. Henceforward, this new and important significance of drawing is valid for European art without detriment to its former functions.

Drawing maintained all these functions in Rembrandt's work. He was one of the most intensive and productive draughtsmen in the history of

Western art. But drawing meant something else to him, something unknown in earlier periods. Drawings by Rembrandt which were projects for compositions, single studies for details of compositions painted or etched afterwards, or gifts for particular occasions, are comparatively few in number. The greater part consists either of studies from life, or of what might be called "drawn monologues". To the latter belong almost all the representations of biblical and historical subjects. To explain the new significance these drawings originally had for their own creator, an earlier example of the kind must be considered. This new significance of drawing began to be developed in the second half of the sixteenth century, with some rare anticipators in the fifteenth century such as Hieronymus Bosch. Pieter Bruegel the Elder left a lot of studies which he himself entitled as "done from the living model". A sheet of a sketch-book (fig. 2), representing a peasant resting on his walk to market (Tolnay, No. 108),[1] is not an isolated fragment of picture anatomy but a bit of breathing life. We understand him in his heavy, ponderous, strongminded quality, appearing like a piece of the earth he works, with all the weightiness and thoughtfulness of Flemish people. The master generally added written colour notes to his studies from life and it would be tempting to suppose that he did so in order to use the colours in his paintings. But that was rarely the case. The drawings became for the artist a source of recollection and life-illusion which he needed for producing similar creatures on his panels out of his creative imagination. The colour notes were intended to increase the liveliness of this inner vision.

For Rembrandt, most of his drawings served to stimulate his imagination. His artistic ideas and conceptions were in a state of constant evolution and development, changing indefatigably and procreating new forms, new solutions. Constantijn Huygens, the Governor's secretary, one of Rembrandt's first Maecenases, admired in him as a young man this restlessness of artistic thinking and working. It was caused by a deep giftedness of Rembrandt's artistic character. Never satisfied with an attainment, with a solution, he moulded his ideas and inventions further and further, giving them ever new appearances. The unfolding of the artistic idea itself becomes no less a work of art than its single embodiments. This unfolding is, without prejudice to its quality of unceasing further development, accomplished and organically completed in every single stage. By virtue of this quality, many of Rembrandt's most fugitive drawings become complete works of art. We must keep this in mind while observing Rembrandt's development as a draughtsman.

It is easy to understand that Rembrandt in his beginning followed the

[1] Charles de Tolnay, *Die Zeichnungen Pieter Bruegels*. Zürich 1952.

6

principles familiar to the practice of the school he derived from. This practice is, through his master Pieter Lastman, linked with Italian art, and in a way academic. The Roman realism of the early seventeenth century, formed by Caravaggio and his most important northern follower, Adam Elsheimer, was decisive for the style of the artists from whom Rembrandt proceeded: Lastman, Jan and Jacob Pynas, and Mœyaert. Of chief importance to him, besides these Dutch followers of Caravaggio and Elsheimer, were the painters of the Utrecht school, Italianists and followers of Caravaggio also. The paintings of the first years of his activity show him starting from the premises furnished by these artists. A painting in the Melbourne Gallery representing *Two Philosophers in Discussion* surrounded by a wonderful still-life of books, dated 1628 (fig. 3), shows him in close contact with Bloemaert, Honthorst and Terbruggen, surpassing all of them in vigorous power and monumentality. These are the personal qualities of Rembrandt's work, the manner of its coming to birth was just the same as theirs. The Italianists adopted the Southern manner. At first they invented an abstract composition and realized it afterwards by building it up from details studied carefully from the living model. The model was posed in the attitude needed for a certain figure and the whole composition was built up, realized, from such details which we may compare to the stones of a building. Rubens in his early years was an Italianist too and proceeded in the same way. Although the young Rembrandt refused, as Huygens reports, to travel to Italy because he did not want to lose the time necessary for his work, he was nevertheless disposed to receive the lessons Italian art was able to teach him, since he himself emphasized that Holland's collections were rich enough in Italian paintings to learn from.

A drawing in the Berlin Print Room (No. 2) gives a good idea of Rembrandt's docility to the teaching of the artists of the older, Italy-bound generation. The sitter, a long-bearded *Old Man with a Book*, was put in the posture needed for the picture. The drawing is a perfect example of Rembrandt's earliest style. It is done with red and black chalk, a technique much in favour among the Utrecht painters. Its careful execution is the absolute graphic parallel to the heavy, tough, tenacious handling of the brush in Rembrandt's early paintings. The man is enveloped in clothes of thick woven stuffs which increase his weightiness. He weighs heavily, presses down on the ground. He forms a compact silhouette like mediaeval drapery figures, the outlines of which are nowhere interrupted. The artist tries to avoid all sharp accents liable to disturb this compactness; thus he shows the head in half profile. At the same time we are able to observe the intensity and carefulness of Rembrandt's modelling, comparable only to Old Netherlandish art of the Late Gothic period.

Fig. 1. Callot: *The Raising of the Cross.*
Etching.

The artistic current from which Rembrandt derived was in his time not at all the predominant one. With its intention of rendering an ideal poetical or historical world by realistic means, it was already in decline, eclipsed by the new naturalism aiming at giving only a true picture of the real Dutch world and Dutch life. This current was in a way still bound in the convention of Italianism and Mannerism. The most important Western etcher and draughtsman at this time was the Frenchman Jacques Callot, who started a new era of graphic expression, not only in his native country, where one of his most spirited followers was Claude Vignon, but abroad as well. So there was in Holland between 1620 and 1630 a strong wave of Callot influence, to be seen not only in superficial imitators, second-rank etchers like Jan Porcellis and Gillis van Scheyndel, but to be felt as a deep essential approach in the aims of the representative personalities of the younger generation as well. The most important among them was Rembrandt. A drawing like the *Raising of the Cross* (No. 1) in the Museum Boymans at Rotterdam shows Rembrandt clearly on the path of a draughtsman such as Callot. The conception is a very old one; it derives from German art of the early sixteenth century, especially from Altdorfer. It played an important part in sixteenth-century Netherlandish art as well, and was transmitted to the period of Rubens and Rembrandt by the etching of Callot, *The Raising of the Cross*, Lieure 548[1] (fig. 1). In rising silhouette figures Callot reanimates the flamboyant style of Late Gothic times. Figures of this kind can be seen in this drawing as well: the commander forming the top of the composition, and the spectators and lansquenets in the background rising against the sky with their spears, halberds and fantastically plumed hats. In such features the vertical tendency familiar to Late Mannerism as well as to Late Gothic art finds expression. Moreover we are able to recognize in this drawing some advance derived from Callot's brilliant style of "short-hand" drawing as well, if we may use this expression. The sudden jumping of tender, delicate hair-lines into strong shadowy ones, giving the bodies a certain flat relief, is a manner created by Callot. Callot's skill in fixing the rapidity of dramatic emotion in a graphic

1 J. Lieure, *Jacques Callot. Catalogue de l'Oeuvre gravé.* 3 vols. Paris 1927.

8

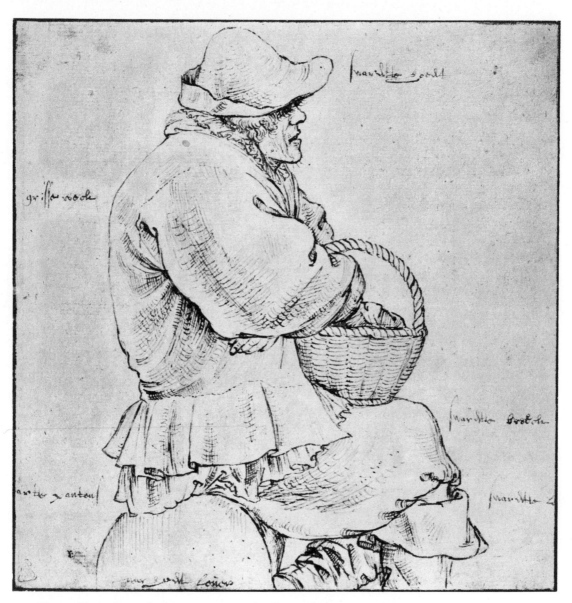

Fig. 2. Pieter Bruegel: *Peasant resting on his Way to Market*. Pen and bistre. Vienna, Albertina.

Fig. 3. Rembrandt: *Two Philosophers in Discussion*. 1628. Melbourne, National Gallery of Victoria.

Fig. 4. Rembrandt: *St. Peter and St. John healing the Paralysed at the Gate of the Temple*. About 1629. Etching.

Fig. 5. Rembrandt: *Abraham's Sacrifice*. 1635. Leningrad, Hermitage.

way was very likely to inspire a young artist. Needless to say Rembrandt gave a deep sense of reality to all that was only decorative, calligraphic in Callot's work. One of the chief means which enabled Rembrandt to do so, was his masterly treatment of light. Composition of light: bright surfaces and spaces full of light opposed to figures moving in half-shadow play an important part in the *Raising of the Cross*. Light removes in Rembrandt's works all restraints of studio-convention and manneristic formalism. The world of historical imagination became for him a world he had experienced in real life. He got his imagination out of observation of real life. That is Rembrandt's quite personal creative power, which enabled him to revolutionize the old academic convention.

In the sixteen-twenties, still working in his native town Leiden in the same studio with his friend and earliest companion Jan Lievens, he used to draw and to etch old beggars from life, figures of misery, familiar to those warlike times, in Jacques Callot's France no less than in Rembrandt's Holland. Young Rembrandt's favourite tool for drawing was soft red or black chalk giving a stroke full of light and colour. About the year 1628 he drew a series of large beggar studies (e.g. Benesch 31), most brilliant perceptions of nature. With these drawings the young artist enters the rank of the first masters and becomes the only equal to Rubens in the Netherlands. As a momentary vision an old man with his humble deprecating gesture steps out of misty space gleaming with light (No. 3). This feature, characteristic of all Dutch art, that everything is not a detached and isolated fragment as in Italian art, but seen together with the totality of atmospheric space surrounding it, finds in Rembrandt's art its most sublime development. Light was in his early years the element by which Rembrandt achieved the illusion of space. In his later years there were added still other elements which we shall have to discuss later. The strokes of the present drawing are hurrying to follow the imaginative perception of the artist, and it seems to grow under our eyes. This drawing is a good example of how early Rembrandt inverted the process of artistic creation in contrast to his precursors. Out of the perception of reality rose the imagination of a biblical event. The deep impression which this humble figure made on him became for Rembrandt the vision of St. Peter healing the paralysed at the temple door, humble instrument of divine grace acting as a miracle-worker. So he used it for a powerful etching (fig. 4).

This manner of acquiring imagination through life experience is a constructive element in Rembrandt's art. In the mirror of reality he perceived his mental world. This world shows his own features. Of no other artist do we know so many self-portraits (No. 20). All the heights and depths of psychical emotion Rembrandt studied first of all in his own face. In a similar way he called into existence the figures of the Bible and profane history through the members of his own family, the miller family in Leyden. Father, mother, brother and sister became for him apostles, philosophers, warriors, prophetesses and fairies, figures of a far remote, bygone, imaginative world, dressed by him in clothes of his own fancy. But this imaginative world was for him the real world of existence and he gave it a vividness surpassing by far the lifelikeness of the contemporary naturalists.

The world of the Bible forms a good part of Rembrandt's work. There was a deep religious sensitivity in him. He was able to translate a fascinating impression of life immediately into biblical vision. Like many others in his youth he tried biblical compositions of several figures; they still show his dependency on his masters Lastman and Pynas (No. 4). Dialogue and mono-logue figures are more in keeping with Rembrandt's genius. These old men, full of dignity, deeply lost in their thoughts, for the Utrecht painters only sitters furnishing them with realistic character-studies, became for Rembrandt St. Paul writing the Pauline Epistles, St. Peter repenting or the prophet Jeremiah mourning on the ruins of Jerusalem. In the years from 1629 to 1631 Rembrandt did a whole series of such studies of old men in red and black chalk (No. 5). Some are dated, forming a starting-point for the pro-blem of chronology. These drawings clearly show the freedom in handling the pencil that Rembrandt had acquired. Curving lines mould the body out of space. One can follow the artist's development of the form. The groping movement of the pencil traces out at first an interior imagination, an almost physical feeling of the model's existence before setting off the definite form. One is able to follow the growth of the feeling in the curving, sloping, groping lines, filled by the porous hatchings indicating the surface of rough stuffs which gives a light transparency to the whole figure. The deepest shadows are set in with vigour, marking with sharp, edged lines, almost engraved in the paper, the main indications of the body's structure. In con-trast to this strongly and intensively drawn part, the head is modelled delicately and subtly, gleaming as though in sunshine, melting with softly waving hair in the atmosphere. Venetian painting was always of highest importance for Netherlandish art. Rembrandt's precursors were no less indebted to it than to Caravaggism. Titian's, Tintoretto's and Bassano's Saints and apostles are the ancestors of so many biblical figures in Dutch art of the second half of the sixteenth and the beginning of the seventeenth century. In his early years Rembrandt received these types probably through intermediaries only. But it is astonishing how closely he approached the originators. These figures are in feeling nearer to the Venetian masters than all those which northern art had brought forth up to this time.

With this drawing we conclude the consideration of the period of Rem-brandt's early youth. It shows the result of intensive efforts. Rembrandt has freed himself from the bonds of Mannerism and Italianism not by denying them as others did, but by reviving them from the inside, by transforming their whole structure and essence. *He had got hold of real life*, and therewith he had found his own way.

The young artist's reputation had grown greatly in the meantime. In the course of the year 1631 Rembrandt was called to Amsterdam to execute portrait orders there. In 1632 he settled there definitely, probably in consequence of the order for the group-portrait of Dr. Tulp and his anatomic audience (Bredius 403). This move to Amsterdam, due to financial considerations, was to be of primary importance in regard to his artistic life also. Amsterdam was then undoubtedly the economic, cultural and artistic centre of the northern countries, the scene of the activity of a large number of artists and art-dealers. Rembrandt had already found his own form; now he was ready to receive plenty of impulses. He stayed at first with the art-dealer Hendrik van Uylenburgh. There he met the latter's cousin, Saskia, a wealthy young lady of patrician birth. This meeting was to be decisive in furthering his life as a man and as an artist. Our special subject does not allow us to recount Rembrandt's biography in detail, but may I recall how Rembrandt's economic situation, changed by his wife's fortune and his new fame as a fashionable portrait-painter with princely fees and plenty of pupils, enabled him to appease his immense hunger for life in all its forms, present and past. It allowed him not only to enjoy the happiness of home and family and to utilize it as an artist (Nos. 6, 7), but to surround himself in fancy with the world of the past by means of the most universal and comprehensive art collection of its time.

One of Rembrandt's most attractive drawings is the *Portrait of Saskia* in the Berlin Print Room (No. 8), a proof of his happiness and enjoyment of life. The lovely girl is represented in summer-dress with a large brimmed straw-hat, holding a flower in her hand. The drawing is the product of a moment of happy inspiration, but shows all the certainty that Rembrandt had won in his mastering of nature. He renders completely a person's spontaneous feeling, unaffected and natural. The great observer of the soul in all its transformations that Rembrandt was, is at work here full-grown. The drawing is done in the favourite technique of the Old Netherlandish masters, with silverpoint, a technique deriving from the goldsmith's practice and allowing a particularly fine, soft and exact modelling, making a drawing a piece of jewellery. Rembrandt used it rarely, only for a few more hasty landscape studies done perhaps on the same occasion. Here it was fitted to the precious subject. Whereas the head is modelled thoroughly, the body is indicated with less care but not less strikingly.

The first half of this decade, when in painting he was occupied with portrait orders, was a time when in etching and drawing he was primarily concerned with large and small biblical compositions (Nos. 10, 11) and with intensive research into nature and reality. Rembrandt was constantly observing, both in the street and at home. His house was situated in the Jewish quarter of Amsterdam, and from his threshold he could watch the most chequered crowd of people of all nations and races one can imagine. From them he chose his models. Indoors he was no less observant. In the documents concerning Rembrandt, there is mentioned a precious portfolio with drawings, representing the *Life of Women*, in Dutch *Vrouwenleven*. It contained many striking and pleasing scenes like *The naughty Boy* (No. 12). Rembrandt's house was filled with young life. There were new-born children – they died at an early age, except the last one – there arrived housemaids, servants and nurses with mothers and other children as models, and we may imagine, that the artist's house sometimes became overcrowded with this "life of women". Rembrandt now preferred the pen as a tool for his drawings and bistre and Indian ink as media. The flexible quill-pen permitted him to follow with rapid, certain strokes the most moving and restless models as we may appreciate here. Studies from life like this were not used as direct preparations, but as sources of inspiration for etched and painted compositions.

The intimate acquaintance with nature and its forms strengthened and enriched the artist's stylistic feeling. That was of advantage for his activity as a portrait painter in which he had not only to undergo the influence but also to endure the competition of the considerable Amsterdam school represented by Thomas de Keyser, Nicolaes Elias and Dirck Santvoort. He adopted their style of representational portrait painting and gave it a new greatness and dignity of appearance. A reflex of this life-sized portrait painting is to be seen in the masterly drawing from the Mrs. Charles Payson Collection, New York (No. 9). Rembrandt has dated it 1634 and signed with his full name, a proof that no further painted execution was planned, but that the drawing itself signifies his artistic aim. It is carefully built up in a mixed technique of red and black chalk, pen and brush with different shades of bistre. It is in this way almost modelled like a painting and has thus the effect of a painting. The sitter is shown in an arm-chair, separated from the spectator by a shadowed wall giving through an arch a view into the bright space containing the model. This is a specifically Baroque feature telling us that this is no narrow and limited object, but an excerpt of the universe of space and light, to which the subject shown also belongs. The spectator is thought to be passing by and to catch a glimpse of the person. The whole conception is not an objective, but a purely subjective one. The picture is directed at the spectator and presupposes his mental readiness to pay attention. Although there is a quite deliberate composition, based on the principle of the triangle, the figure of the man shows the purest freedom from all constraint. It has been suggested that the sitter might have been Constantijn's brother Maurits Huygens, thus a personality of high social rank, but in comparison with Van Dyck's portraits his appearance is unpretentious and human, corresponding to Holland's democratic spirit.

In the years from 1630 to 1640 Rembrandt approached most closely to Baroque art. About 1635–36 is a culminating point showing his art emulating the grandeur and stateliness of Italian art. This emulation is not an external one like that of many contemporaries, but an internal one, a result of his highly developed feeling for the inner monumentality of pictorial form. This feeling may have been brought out and developed also by his specifically Dutch national activity as a painter of large-sized portraits. Now he could use his newly gained experience in the devising of large-sized compositions for re-fashioning the old biblical subjects. Rembrandt, who had started with cabinet-painting, became a real monumental painter, in a way which surprised and troubled his Dutch contemporaries. Never before had there been seen in Dutch art, which inclines to immobility and passivity, such turbulent agitation as Rembrandt showed in his life-sized biblical and mythological paintings. He enjoyed incorporating himself in his favourite hero Samson, challenging the Philistines. *Movement* is one of the most important constituent features of Baroque art; so it was one of the chief problems Rembrandt worked on in this decade. He judges the quality of his own works by the expression of movement attained in them. Heavy, ponderous bodies are moved in sweeping curves, things are observed in a flying and falling state. That means an increase of dramatically emphasized situations. Rembrandt prefers the moments of highest tension, of catastrophic change. *Abraham's Sacrifice* (fig. 5) is represented at the moment when the angel snatches his arm and the terrified patriarch drops the hovering knife. This painting in the Hermitage, dated 1635, makes plain what Rembrandt's artistic aims were at this time. The monumental figures threaten to shatter the frame, which is drawn closely round them in order to increase their vehement plasticity. Rembrandt made a preparatory drawing for this picture, now in the British Museum Print Room (No. 13), which shows in an instructive manner, how he altered his composition whilst evolving an idea. As a matter of fact, the drawing represents a quite different type of composition earlier in style. The three figures are piled with red chalk one above the other like a tower rising to the sky – a feature characteristic of Rembrandt's earliest years (compare No. 4) – every one in the same diagonal posture, surrounded by plenty of space, waving in masses of light and shadow indicated by black chalk and Indian ink. In the painting Rembrandt stressed the contrasts of the bodies to the detriment of the chiaroscuro of space, and

17

spread their plasticity out over the canvas. Both of the conceptions have their specific qualities, are works of art in themselves, and it is significant that the formulation of the drawing was utilized by a pupil in a painting at Munich, corrected by the master himself.

Rembrandt owned among his art treasures a large number of prints and drawings by old masters. How close his inward proximity to Italian art then was may be seen from his copies after Leonardo's *Last Supper*. They are drawn after Lombard engravings of the beginning of the sixteenth century. Rembrandt was seeking Italian art and behind the Baroque he divined the real sources, the great originators of the classic period of the High Renaissance. A mediocre reproduction of the composition enabled him to resuscitate the loftiness and greatness of an original which he had never seen. In a red chalk drawing in the Robert Lehman Collection, New York (Benesch 443), he followed the stiff engraving rather closely. In the Berlin pen drawing (No. 14) – which he was proud of, because he fully signed and dated it 1635 – he soared up from his model and transformed the whole composition, with the result that he gives much more of the spirit and meaning of the original than exact copies ever could. The movement of spiritual excitement goes through the apostles like a surging sea and makes their group undulate like waves. The features of the apostles are only indicated, nevertheless they sparkle with the spiritual life expressed by the movement of the whole body.

Free, invented composition was the strength of old art in contrast to that of our century, where the artist is mostly dependent upon a model. Anybody using pencil or pen who has ever tried to follow the way of creative inventors of past times, must confess how impossible it is to produce in one's own mind this intensity of inward vision which might enable one to transmit it to the blank surface of a sheet of paper. *Invention* was perhaps the foremost quality an artist was asked for in the past. Then, too, it was not everybody's affair. The average artist had to improve on conventional schemes which he had to follow. Only the creative artist revolutionized the schemes by the power of his inner vision and replaced them by a new nearness to life. So Rembrandt did. Brimful of experience of nature and natural form, he was able to realize his conceptions every moment.

Regardless of his humanistic education – his father had intended him to be a scholar and Rembrandt had passed through Latin classes as the preparatory stage of university studies – he was not a great reader. His library was comparatively poor and contained, besides some books by friends and illustrated works, only the Bible. But he read this book over and over again; it became for him the book of real, complete life. Like the great German illustrators before him, he felt the experiences of the Bible as recent events,

18

and he felt them intensively, as though they were experiences in his own life. His sketches of biblical events are so affecting that they give the impression of his having seen them in reality. A person looking at a *Carrying of the Cross* (No. 15) is as terrified and touched as a follower of the procession. Dramatic movement could not be presented more strikingly. Christ has just broken down under His burden, struck by the soldiers, while Veronica, overpowered by grief, faints, and the Holy Women with St. John rush forward to help her. The movement of the penstrokes alone, without regard to their significance, shows excitement. The character of the scene as a subjective impression is increased by the dark, indistinct silhouette of a soldier to the left. Almost twenty years before, the young Van Dyck had drawn similar dramatic Passion scenes. These have been supposed to have influenced Rembrandt; but I think that he was strong enough to arrive at such results on his own.

Besides being the creator of an imaginative world, Rembrandt remained the intensive observer of reality that he always was. His young wife, moving around in their home or staying in bed during her frequent illnesses (Nos. 18, 21, 32), relatives of his family (No. 31), actors on the stage (No. 17), peasants brawling in an inn (No. 19), works of art he saw at the houses of collectors or at sales (Nos. 26, 33), colourful pageants (No. 29) pass by the eye of the spectator who peruses Rembrandt's portfolios. About 1636 he began to observe and to study landscape assiduously in his drawings (Nos. 22, 23), whereas in painting and etching he did not begin before the end of the decade. The draughtsman was always *ahead* in Rembrandt's development. In two drawings in the Budapest Print Room (Benesch 463, 464) he studied the corner of a Dutch cottage. The riper one (No. 23) brings things in a narrow excerpt very near to the spectator; it gives an immensity of growing life in this old stem of a vine climbing on the roofs, blossoming and spreading out in bright sunshine the sparkling waves of its thousandfold leaves. Brooding warmth lies over the scenery, a feeling of summer. The shadows lie dark, and their gloom, alternating with reflections, brings positive glare to the untouched portion of the paper, making it a source of radiant light.

Most of the Dutch painters of the seventeenth century became specialists, each one choosing a special field of subject-matter, in which he excelled and was esteemed by the public. The landscape painters showed in their works the new conception of the universe reflecting in every little part of their native country the infinity of universal space. The same tension between the infinitely small and the infinitely large dominates the natural science of the time.

Rembrandt, the only universalist, was the only one mastering all fields of the specialists. More than all specialists, he fills his landscape drawings with a certain greatness and majesty, however modest may be the natural motif. In the same way his animal drawings show in many respects his absolute superiority over all animal painters. In his drawings of elephants in 1637 (No. 27), he not only gives fullest evidence of the animal's outward appearance, with its wrinkled skin, silvery grey in light, but of its clever character too, expressed by its deliberate movements and the cunning look of its small eyes.

In the second half of the sixteen-thirties Rembrandt drew in his biblical compositions the synthesis of all his previous experiences in the field of free invention and study from nature. The grisaille painting of the *Sermon of St. John the Baptist* (Berlin, fig. 6), to which Rembrandt seems to have attached great value, because his friend Jan Six acquired it in later years and Rembrandt himself then designed a frame for it, is a proof of this no less than the etching of the *Death of the Virgin* (B. 99, Hind 161, Münz 208). Rembrandt revived in the compositions some of the solemnly soaring features of his youth (No. 24), but deployed at the same time all the epic breadth of description of which his intense observation and study of nature made him capable, even when he was not sketching directly after models (No. 25). Thus he gained the admirable concentration which we note in his drawings toward the close of the sixteen-thirties (No. 28), foreshadowing the large projects of the sixteen-forties.

*　　*　　*

After this decade of development of a powerfully-moved Baroque style and of intensive research in all fields of nature, there came at the beginning of the sixteen-forties a surprising change in Rembrandt's manner, decisive for his whole later development.

Although Rembrandt's exaggerated demonstration of power and frightening movement must have shocked the average Dutchman, his artistic aims had not been intended essentially to contrast with prevailing tastes. In a somewhat strange but imposing manner, he had stated what the public wanted to be shown by a modern master. For some years he was even a sort of fashionable painter, in favour with Amsterdam society and with the possibility of becoming a dictator of taste such as Van Dyck was in England. The influence Rembrandt exercised on his surroundings in his first Amsterdam period was, except in the case of his pupils, but a superficial one. The deep significance of his art was even then not wholly understood by his contemporaries. Paradoxical as it may sound for a pioneer such as Rembrandt, his Baroque was old-fashioned and, in a way, out of date. His Baroque is strongly mixed with elements of late Renaissance time, like that of his friend, the famous silversmith Jan Lutma, and has an archaic, historical

Fig. 6. Rembrandt: *The Sermon of St. John the Baptist.* About 1635. Grisaille. Berlin, Staatliche Museen.

Fig. 7. Andrea Mantegna: *The Calumny of Apelles*. Pen and bistre. London, British Museum.

Fig. 8. Antonio Tempesta: *Diana and Actaeon*. Etching.

appearance, inclining to mediaeval mysteriousness and loftiness. Rembrandt was always strange to his surroundings, and the discordance between his own and public artistic opinion soon became evident. So he turned away from what his time expected of him and pursued his own aims. He became no painter flattering society like Van Dyck, he did not change his heavy Baroque to fashionable gracefulness, on the contrary he strengthened its architectonic character. Rembrandt was intensely interested in architecture – we know that from his library. In the beginning of the sixteen-forties he increased not only the importance of architectural scenery in his works, but gave to the whole composition an architectonic character. The fantastic buildings in his paintings, their heavy truncated towers and large masses of stone correspond in a way to English architectural feeling. It is significant that Rembrandt drew at this time, after engravings or drawings, views of old English towns: London, Windsor, St. Albans. The most brilliant of these copies, which is in the Berlin Print Room (No. 36), is a *View of London*, with Old St. Paul's in the centre. The divination of English architectural feeling manifested by Rembrandt in this drawing is admirable: the majestic rising of the cathedral in evening-light above the shadowy, jumbled masses of old buildings. Avoiding details and only by the rectangular rhythms of pen-strokes with supporting contrasts of light and dark, Rembrandt not only completely renders the hilly movement of English landscape formation, but the tessellated, perpendicular character of English town building as well. The divination of nature and reality in the flowing greatness of this conception of space is so intense that one might suppose Rembrandt to have been in England. But it is quite a different thing to portray landscape from reality. Whereas in his paintings about this time Rembrandt developed visionary landscapes continuing Hercules Seghers' style, in etchings and drawings like *Cottages before a Stormy Sky*, Albertina (No. 37), he discovered homely nature – the features of the Dutch countryside, with men going to their work and women with children. Rembrandt's fondness for tectonic structure, for substantiality in everything seen in landscape is expressed in this drawing as well. It was done just at the same time as Rembrandt etched his famous *Windmill* and his landscapes with cottages.

This specific quality becomes visible now throughout all compositions, in the *Night Watch* no less than in the beginning of the *Hundred Guilder Print* which Rembrandt commenced about 1640 (No. 34). One knows that the former signifies an external change in Rembrandt's career as well. The spiritualization of Baroque pomp, splendour and movement in the *Night Watch*, the transfiguration of a civil performance into a world beyond – the persons portrayed seem to come out of their tombs – the strange unusual architecture of the whole composition, induced the public to withdraw their favour from the artist, a fact which finally led to Rembrandt's economic ruin. How he arrived at such a composition must have been a strange thing for the Dutch.

Compositional drawings from the beginning of the sixteen-forties show this new striving for balance and tectonic firmness (Nos. 35, 38, 39) as well, without detriment to the inner dramatic life which fills them. About the middle of the decade he developed that abstract method of drawing for the layout of compositions (No. 46) which was to become an essential element in clarifying his style of drawing in the sixteen-fifties.

The new firmness attained by Rembrandt was followed by a general calming down. His paintings unfold a new beauty of colour and light in which the drawings also participate (No. 40). The vehement movement slows down. The dramatic excitement becomes inward tension. Biblical stories become quieter and deeper (No. 42). A drawing which represents *The Brethren of Joseph requesting Benjamin* (No. 43) relating to old Jacob their astonishing adventures in Egypt, is a typical specimen of Rembrandt's style about 1645. The eldest brother is speaking, the others are listening thoughtfully, among them little Benjamin. Rembrandt drew this subject twice and modelled it intensively. The penstroke has lost its hurrying, violent dynamism. Lines go in quiet curves, sliding, turning and returning, circumscribing the coloured surface.

Rembrandt endeavours in his drawings of the second half of the decade to attain the rich effect of his palette. The surfaces of all things in nature have a new interest for him, their quality as material of relation to their colouristic importance. The study of a nude young man in the Albertina, used for an etching about 1646, develops the illuminated figure out of a whole symphony of different shadows of brown and grey wash, silvery grey heightenings with body-colour. Brush, sharp quill- and broad reed-pen are working confusedly to attain a rich and picturesque totality. These drawings represent perhaps the summit of Rembrandt's chiaroscuro principle. He tries not only to give material evidence of the surface of a cloth, as in the portrait-drawing of 1634, but to give *colour*, and so he goes further inwards, penetrates the surface. In this way he catches, so to speak, more of the subject's soul (Nos. 48, 49). That is to be seen in a very impressive way also in the drawings he did about 1647 of little old towns on his way to Gelderland. A drawing of the *Western Gate at Rhenen* (No. 54) renders not only a fascinating, picturesque totality, but gives more: the sentiment of past times, of a declined world, the secret beauty of ruin and decay. The quiet greatness of this architecture with its emphasis on vertical and horizontal line shows the far-reaching change Rembrandt's manner of thinking and *planning* had undergone. His drawings of Dutch scenery breathe the same spirit (No. 55).

At the end of the sixteen-forties Rembrandt turned definitively away from the Baroque ideals of his youth, from outer movement, sharp accents, and emphasized character (No. 51, 52). His art becomes quiet and silent, concentrated on the essential in great simple forms, discovering the internal structure of spirit and existence. The line has more concentration, in highly dramatic and emotional scenes also (No. 53). He continues his solitary way, followed only by a little group of pupils and admirers, entirely understood by no one.

* * *

It is remarkable that the following decade, the time of Rembrandt's mature and late style – the culmination of Dutch art likewise – is especially rich in the production of drawings. Drawing as a special artistic medium is only now developed in full. It becomes of particular importance as a medium through which Rembrandt can most immediately and intensely give visible form to his thoughts (Nos. 56, 59, 60, 61, 62). Thus drawing strongly influenced the tenor of painting and etching. That is to be seen in the simplest study from nature, like a chalk drawing of a *Man seated* (No. 57). How strongly closed, how simple and monumental these rhythms have become appears by comparison with the beggar studies done twenty-two years earlier (No. 3). In spite of his strong movement in space, the figure is more compact, and his limbs are joined at right angles to each other. The outlines confine a clear silhouette, yet nevertheless breathe and fluctuate with colour. The features are indicated only by the broad outlines, but completely render the nature and condition of this thoughtful man. The figure is full of atmosphere, but atmosphere is now a quality of mind.

That becomes evident in the landscape drawings as well. The beginning of the sixteen-fifties were the years of Rembrandt's most intensive landscape studies. Troubles and difficulties in the lonely man's life induced him to seek recreation outside the gates of Amsterdam. He only now realizes the majestic immensity of homely nature, in which he no longer needs fantastic vision to express his feeling of the universe. He does not any longer need heavy contrasts of dark and light to create space. Space rises out of the rhythms of the penstrokes only, and some few half-shadows and light washes give the modelling infinite softness. The leaves of the trees wave in a calm breeze, and air circulates through the branches (No. 66). Here Rembrandt found also the clearest formulation of nature, and it is interesting to see how closely he approaches to landscape drawings of Titian and his followers which were well known to him (Nos. 63, 75). Rembrandt has turned back to the classic art of the sixteenth century. In their last formulations, great masters always acknowledge the same profound laws of existence. Rembrandt had his favourite excursions outside of Amsterdam: along the banks of the Amstel river and on the Amstelveensche Weg (Nos. 77, 78). The latter he has shown in a drawing, so imposing in all its simplicity, with the *Huys met het Toorentje* rising among the lightly swaying branches of trees covered with the first tiny leaves of spring (No. 67). All details are indicated with an old master's exactitude, and here again Rembrandt approached quite close to the preceding century's greatest northern follower of the Venetian masters: Pieter Bruegel. But what matters is not the details, it is rather the quiet, floating movement of space in the luminous immensity of the open air.

The retrospective tendency in Rembrandt's classic art led him back to the masters of the Renaissance and of classic antiquity. The figure of Homer impressed him deeply; again and again he moulded the idea of the blind seer, which had come down to him through antique copies and casts. In the family album of his friend, Doctor Joannes Six, he drew *Homer on Parnassus reciting Verses* (No. 64). He was inspired in this instance by the composition of Raphael's fresco in the Stanze of the Vatican. This drawing, dated 1652, gives a perfect notion of Rembrandt's mature style of figure composition. All curves are avoided. The figures are composed of cubes, rhombs and cylindrical forms, and have a clearly crystallized shape. Sometimes their abstractness gives them the appearance of articulated dolls. Yet they are far from being lifeless. On the contrary, the simplicity of their shape, and their external immobility increases their inner vitality. With a minimum of means a maximum of expression is attained. Deep affection takes hold of the poet's silent audience. The faces are generalized, but the attitude of the bodies expresses their feelings. In similar manner, only by the rhythms of pure line, without supporting washes, Rembrandt gives the perfect illusion of space and light – one of the greatest secrets of his late art.

This drawing is a classic specimen too of Rembrandt's mature pen technique. The master preferred in his late period the reed-pen to the quill-pen. The nature of this instrument with its cut point tends to encourage the drawing of straight lines joining at right angles (Nos. 74, 75, 76, 79). When drawn in the direction of its length, it gives a strong, broad line; drawn transversely, it gives a very fine and sharp one. This alternation of strong and fine lines was used by Rembrandt to obtain the highest degree of picturesque illusion. It corresponds completely to his brushwork, which, with its large and free handling, resembles the bold movement of the reed-pen (Nos. 82, 83, 84, 85). The culminating point of this technique is around 1655–56. It is comparable to the brushwork of the mature Titian, and never before was Rembrandt's proximity to Titian so great as now. One may remember the magnificence of the female figures like "Bathsheba" in the Louvre, the grandness of portraits like the "Jan Six" in Amsterdam, and one will realize

Fig. 9. Rembrandt: *The Conspiracy of Julius Civilis*. About 1661. Stockholm, Nationalmuseum.

Fig. 10. Rembrandt: *The Syndics of the Clothmakers' Guild* ("De Staalmeesters"). 1662. Amsterdam, Rijksmuseum.

that Rembrandt, starting from his own problems, arrived at a position of true kinship with Titian. One of the most beautiful examples of this kind among his drawings is the *Self-Portrait in Studio Attire* (No. 81) in the Rembrandt House at Amsterdam, showing the master in his working clothes. Arrestingly, he steps in front of the spectator, a silent and attentive observer, most attractive in his firmness of character and human kindness. The simplicity of conception is quite close to Titian's portrait composition as well as to mediaeval figures of northern art. The diagonal strokes of the reed-pen seem to enclose the figure in atmosphere and coloured space. In an incomparable manner Rembrandt renders the colouristic appearance by means of a uniform liquid, dark brown bistre, applied in varying strengths with nothing but the reed-pen. But Rembrandt knew how to draw with the brush quite as well. A powerful drawing of a *Girl sleeping* in the British Museum (No. 86) is radiant with colour. The drawing was done very quickly, and the brush-strokes are like sword-cuts, yet with infinite firmness form is seized and fixed, without need of any pentimenti. In just the same way Rembrandt built up a painting, and the drawing is the immediate parallel to the portraits of the same young girl and of Rembrandt's second wife Hendrickje, done in 1655 and 56. Surpassing all pictorial mastery is the deep spiritual expression, the quiet power of sleep which has seized this young creature.

Rembrandt's idea of giving austere simplicity to human shape was realized in Indian miniatures of the Mogul School of the sixteenth and of the beginning of the seventeenth century. The archaic grace of the precious figures fascinated him so strongly that he copied them in thoroughly executed drawings (Nos. 87, 88), touching the silky surface of warm-coloured Japanese paper with subtle pen-strokes, delicate washes in greyish brown and a few spots of red. More frequently than before Rembrandt now copied exotic and old works of art. He penetrated into them, seized them wholly, if they answered his own artistic purposes, so that he made them quite his own, and that without changing their external appearance so much as he did before. As a further example may serve a drawing by Andrea Mantegna (fig. 7), the severity of which combined with delicacy appealed much to him (No. 89). His universality becomes here visible as well.

Christianity was one of the foremost and essential problems with which the late Rembrandt dealt in his art. Rembrandt's professed religion was Mennonitism, a denomination teaching baptism of adults as an act of personal conviction, in contrast to the predestination dogma of the Calvinist State religion. This persuasion needs personal conviction and draws with it a subjective standpoint to Christian revelation. We know that Rembrandt's religious works reflected this religious subjectivism. But it would be wrong to imagine this religious subjectivism to be nothing but a reflex of Protestant sect-partiality. His Christianity is Christian faith, simply, and it is as universal as his whole spiritual disposition was. His mother was Catholic by birth. We meet in Rembrandt's late work with many figures of Catholic faith: the Holy Virgin and Saints. The solemn, mysterious appearance of these figures he imbued with the ardour of his soul and human depth. Bible stories and Passion scenes of the second half of the sixteen-fifties have the solemnity and sacral remoteness of acts of worship. Thus, they are inspired with a devotion, with a depth of sentiment beyond comparison with that in the early works. Scenes of the New Testament (Nos. 91, 92, 95–98) now predominate over those of the Old, more familiar to Calvinist Holland.

The intention of thick lines in Rembrandt's late drawings is not to make a heavily-marked separation from the mysterious medium of space. On the contrary, it means all the more intensive union with the atmosphere. The atmosphere is, so to speak, banked up on the figures' outlines and becomes visible in dark borders. The figures on the other hand change their substance and become embodiments of atmospheric space, now more a metaphysical medium than a physical one. This may be seen in the Stockholm drawing of the *Arrest of Christ* (No. 98), done about 1660. All physical movement has disappeared. The figures are petrified in their action like mediaeval cathedral sculptures. Yet in the same degree the psychical tension is raised, expressing the moment when the officers become paralysed by Christ's magic power and cannot move a limb.

From the last period of Rembrandt's activity, there are but few drawings known. This is not due to the fact of fewer drawings being preserved, although Rembrandt may have been more careless in keeping his drawings, which he sometimes sketched on the backs of printed leaflets. The preparatory designs for his most imposing and monumental composition of history, *The Conspiracy of Julius Civilis* (fig. 9), he drew on little scraps of paper, one of which is a funeral announcement (No. 100). But we may attribute the lack of drawings from Rembrandt's last years first of all to the fact that drawing as a whole played a less important part in his work after 1661. For the same reason etching disappeared from his production after the same date. Did drawing lose importance for the old Rembrandt, who had turned away from the outer world to become absorbed in the problems of painting, in which colour was no longer a reflection of reality, but a moving principle of being? As a technical process, drawing with pen and pencil on paper really lost importance for Rembrandt. But as a *spiritual* process it became of greater importance to him than ever. Drawing in its deepest sense is handwriting, an immediate emanation of personality, of its rhythm of life and its creative faculty. The greater, the more experienced an artist is, the simpler will be his means of artistic expression. He avoids the roundabout methods of complicated and refined technical processes. The simplest ones, which give direct expression of personality, are just the right ones. This immediateness of drawing, of handwriting, the old Rembrandt caught in his paintings. His pictures contain all the deep wisdom of a man grown old and forsaken in his struggle against the tragic fate of genius unrecognized by his time and surroundings. The expression of the late paintings of Rembrandt would not be so human and stirring, if the colours were not so direct an emanation of feeling and character. This was only to be attained by a technique keeping the whole spontaneity of handwriting, of drawing, a technique as singular, mysterious and impenetrable, as it is simple and uncomplicated. The feeling of immediate handwriting in this brushwork is already contained in the rare drawings we know of this time. Pen and brush give them the radiating power of paint (No. 101).

The old Rembrandt could dispense with all that strangeness and unusualness of appearance, exemplified so markedly in the *Nightwatch* which shocked his contemporaries. In the group-portrait of the *Staalmeesters* (The Syndics of the Clothmakers' Guild), of 1662, nothing can have shocked his customers; nevertheless it is Rembrandt in the fullest expression of his personality (fig. 10). The brushwork of this picture shows all the animation and nervousness of his drawings. On the other hand, the preparatory study of the *Standing Syndic* (No. 102) in the Museum Boymans already contains in its radiating power the complete idea of pictorial totality. Here it may be seen that *drawing* is the key to Rembrandt's whole art, the moving principle of every form of artistic communication, painting and etching included. This drawing, executed with brush and pen, working with body-colours and erasures, is far removed from any graphic system like the drawings and etchings of Rembrandt's very beginnings. But now the master is able to renounce all graphic systems; he is in need of them no longer, as every little stroke contains the power of the creator.

A peculiarity of the seventeenth century was the memorial books, albums filled with tokens of sympathy, friendship and devotion. Distinguished travellers carried such albums with them, asking celebrities they visited for written or drawn records. Scholars and families of social rank submitted them to their friends for the same purpose. Rembrandt also was asked for such remembrances at several occasions. *Homer on the Parnassus* is a folio in the album Pandora of the Six family, the kindred of the famous burgomaster of Amsterdam, Rembrandt's friend. In 1662 Rembrandt drew a little composition in the album of Jacobus Heyblock, a minister of the Dutch church, which is preserved at the Royal Library at the Hague (No. 105). It shows the *Presentation in the Temple*: the old High Priest Simeon receiving in his arms the Child Jesus. From his early youth on, Rembrandt had often represented this episode, one of the most moving and touching of the New Testament. It gave him an opportunity to develop a rich group of figures in the majesty of solemn temple architecture surrounded by crowds of people. The old Rembrandt does away with all this rich *mise en scène*. He shows only Mary, Joseph and Simeon holding the Child. This drawing gives still more striking evidence of the technique of drawing of the late Rembrandt. The whole is an iridescent texture, a waving of shadow and light out of which the figures rise like visions. Intercrossing streams of light, made visible by strokes with a half-dry brush not completely covering the bright ground of the porous paper, alternate with hair-lines of the reed-pen so delicate that they look like formations of brittle glass. White heightening – partly blackened in the course of time as for instance on the head of the Child – is intended to increase the radiant splendour. A large ray falls from heaven almost dissolving the figures of Mary and Joseph, incandescent themselves from the light of their halos. So Simeon remains almost alone, closing his eyes before the outer world like the blind seer Homer drawn and painted so often by Rembrandt, because he perceived the light of the world by his inner sight. It is almost a miracle how the old Rembrandt by dissolving the outer consistency of figures raises their inward reality. There can hardly be found anything more real in art than this patriarch in whom the expression of immense age becomes the expression of immense kindness and bliss. Rembrandt's mastery of light brings this miracle about. There is nothing besides light in this drawing as the shadows too become dark flames.

The very last examples of Rembrandt's draughtsmanship cannot be dated exactly to a year because we lack any chain of chronological development. They are broadly drawn with the reed-pen and may have been done about 1665 but earlier or later as well. The art of drawing seems here to reach its utmost possibilities of expression. *St. Peter at the Death-Bed of Tabitha* (No. 103) is overwhelming through the archetypal significance of the signs set down with the pen on the white surface of the paper, which embodies the idea of the cosmic infinity of space pregnant with form. Rembrandt with his drawing tool is, so to say, fathoming the imaginary structure of his object. Where points of contact arise, the circuit of forces is closed and becomes visible like the lines of a cardiogram.

The drawing of *Diana surprised by Actaeon* (No. 104) is a copy after an indifferent etching by the Italian Antonio Tempesta (fig. 8). The chief figures of this composition were used by Rembrandt for a vision quite of his own. The synthetic style of the *Arrest of Christ* in Stockholm (No. 98), where the figures had broad simplified outlines, begins anew to fluctuate, to oscillate, but not in order to present a pictorial totality as would have been Rembrandt's intention twenty years earlier, but to lay bare the innermost laws of existence. The vibrations of these split penstrokes, of these floating washes, make all bulk diaphanous, dissolve all solid forms. But the result is not a decomposition, as on the other hand space and fluid atmosphere show a tendency to crystallize. In this way a firmness is attained which greatly surpasses that in all the earlier works of Rembrandt. We look into the picture space as into a crystal creating shapes and patterns according to the changing incidence of the rays of light.

This quality of Rembrandt's draughtsmanship of being expression of the creative personality was too revolutionary to be understood by his contemporaries. Rembrandt is the most striking example of the tragic discordance between the artist and his time, so significant for the later centuries of European art. Henceforward not the mere perfection of a work of art in an external sense became the aim of artistic effort, but perfection in the internal one: a work of art must be a self-contained organism. Rembrandt has stated with his drawings a new conception of artistic completeness. A work of art is highly finished if it gives expression to its creator's full personality. In this way a little drawing may be more finished than an overcompleted and overcharged picture. All great draughtsmen of the following centuries – Watteau and Goya, Delacroix and Cézanne – try to keep in their most elaborate works the immediateness and spontaneity of the diagram of mind that drawing means. We may affirm in all justice that it was Rembrandt, the greatest master of modern times, who was the creator of this most fundamental quality of the artistic epoch to which we ourselves belong.

Fig. 11. Rembrandt: *Head of a Bearded Old Man.*
About 1633–4. Pen and bistre.
New York, János Scholz.

NOTE ON THIS EDITION
AND ACKNOWLEDGEMENTS

THE selection from Rembrandt's drawn oeuvre entitled "Rembrandt Selected Drawings", which preceded my critical and chronological catalogue in six volumes, was already out of print when the late Dr. Bela Horovitz, Director of the Phaidon Press, whose untiring enthusiasm furthered the large project, suggested that I should prepare another selective edition after the completion of the large catalogue. This new edition was to serve primarily the purposes of the student and the art-lover, and its principal aim was to be educational. I accepted the idea most eagerly, being convinced that real progress in the field of learning is only achieved through guidance towards a deeper understanding. The result is here submitted to the public. The scientific references, which are of interest only to the specialist, have been replaced by brief notes of interpretation and appreciation. The examples have been chosen from the material of the large corpus, with special regard to their quality and significance. I took the opportunity, however, of including several characteristic drawings discovered since the completion of the corpus. These are published here for the first time.

I am indebted to Mr. Giles Robertson of the University of Edinburgh for the stylistic revision of the Introduction, which is an elaboration of ideas first put forward in a lecture I gave at Harvard University in December 1940 under the auspices of Professor Paul J. Sachs. – My wife has been of great assistance to me in the preparation of this edition, as in all my previous work on Rembrandt.

O. B.

PLATES

1. *The Raising of the Cross*. About 1627-8. Black chalk. Rotterdam, Museum Boymans/Van Beuningen.

2. *Old Man with a Book, seated in Profile to Right, full-length.* About 1628. Red and black chalk, heightened with white. Berlin, Kupferstichkabinett.

3. *Old Man with his Arms extended*. About 1629. Black chalk. Dresden, Kupferstichkabinett.

4. *The Entombment of Christ*. 1630. Red chalk, heightened with white. London, British Museum.

5. *Old Man with Clasped Hands, seated in an Arm-Chair, full-length.* About 1631. Red and black chalk.
Berlin, Kupferstichkabinett.

6. *Young Woman at her Toilet*. About 1632-4. Pen and bistre, washed in bistre and Indian ink. Vienna, Albertina.

7. *Portrait of Saskia standing*. About 1633. Pen and brush in bistre. London, Hugh N. Squire.

8. *Saskia in a Straw Hat*. 1633. Silver-point on white prepared vellum.
Berlin, Kupferstichkabinett.

9. *Gentleman in an Arm-Chair, seen through a Window-Frame.* 1634. Red and black chalk, pen and wash, on vellum. New York, Mrs. Charles S. Payson.

19. *The Raising of the Daughter of Jairus.* About 1632-3. Pen and bistre. Formerly Rotterdam, F. Koenigs Collection.

11. *Jesus and His Disciples.* 1634. Black and red chalk, pen and bistre, washes, heightenings in gouache. Haarlem, Teyler Museum.

12. *The Naughty Boy*. About 1635. Pen and bistre, wash, white body-colour, some black chalk.
Berlin, Kupferstichkabinett.

13. *Abraham's Sacrifice*. About 1635. Red and black chalk, wash in Indian ink, heightened with white, on greenish yellow paper. London, British Museum.

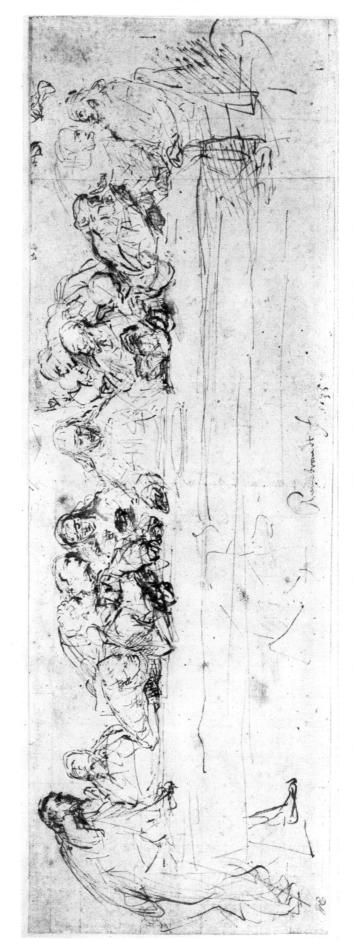

14. *The Last Supper*, after Leonardo da Vinci. 1635. Pen and bistre, wash, white body-colour. Berlin, Kupferstichkabinett.

15. *Christ carrying the Cross*. About 1635. Pen and bistre, wash. Berlin, Kupferstichkabinett.

16. *Study for the Great Jewish Bride.* About 1635. Pen and Indian ink, wash. Stockholm, Nationalmuseum.

17. *Actor on the Stage with a Parrot on his right Shoulder, standing in Front of the Curtain;*
below: a Spectator clapping. About 1635. Pen and bistre. Vienna, Albertina.

Renbrant.

18. *Saskia asleep in Bed.* About 1635. Pen and brush in bistre. Oxford, Ashmolean Museum.

19. *A Brawl of Peasants in an Inn.* About 1637. Pen and bistre, wash. Montpellier, Musée Fabre.

20. *Self-Portrait in Cloak and large Barett, bust.* About 1636. Pen and wash, in bistre and Indian ink.
Formerly New York, Dr. A. Hamilton Rice.

21. *Saskia carrying Rumbartus* (?) *down stairs.* About 1636. Pen and bistre, wash.
New York, Pierpont Morgan Library.

22. *Farm-House amid a Copse.* About 1636. Pen and bistre, wash. Vienna, Bibliothek der Akademie der Bildenden Künste.

23. *Farm-House in Sunlight*. About 1636. Pen and wash. Budapest, Museum of Fine Arts.

34. *St. John the Baptist preaching.* About 1627. Quill-pen (perhaps also reed-pen) and wash in bistre. Private Collection.

25. *Studies for Groups and Figures* in "St. John the Baptist preaching". About 1637. Pen and bistre. Berlin, Kupferstichkabinett.

26. *Susanna and the Elders*. About 1637. Red chalk. Berlin, Kupferstichkabinett.

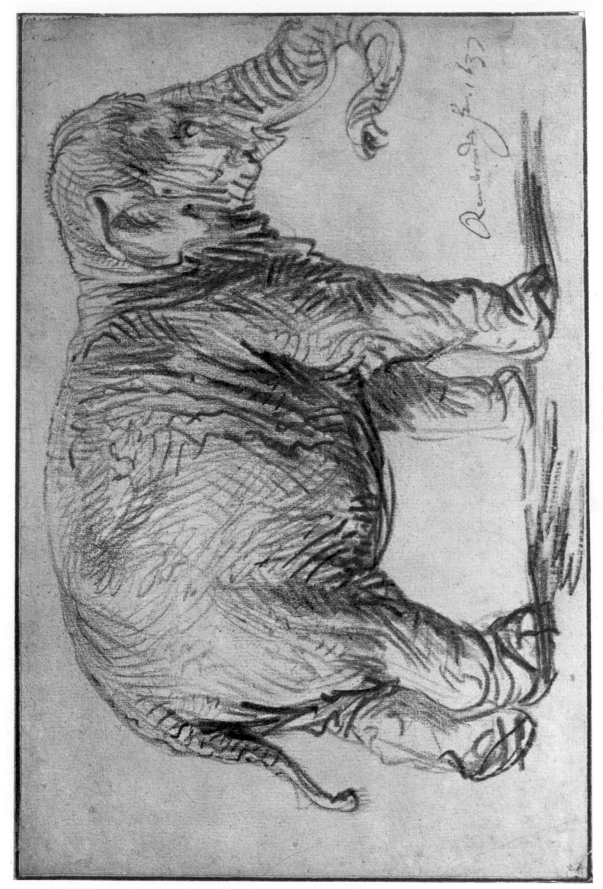

27. *An Elephant.* 1637. Black chalk. Vienna, Albertina.

28. *The Good Samaritan attending to the Wounded Man.* About 1637. Pen and bistre.
Barnsley Park, Cirencester, Lord Faringdon.

29. *Two Negro Drummers mounted on Mules*. About 1637-8. Pen and wash in bistre, coloured with red chalk and yellow water-colour, heightened with white, some oil colour. London, British Museum.

30. *Female Nude with a Snake* (*probably Cleopatra*). About 1637. Red chalk. London, Villiers David.

31. *Titia van Uylenburch*. 1639. Pen and bistre. Stockholm, Nationalmuseum.

32. *Saskia's Lying-in Room.* About 1639. Pen and bistre, washes in bistre and Indian ink, heightened with white. The Hague, F. Lugt.

33. *Baldassare Castiglione*, after Raphael. 1639. Pen and bistre, some white body-colour. Vienna, Albertina.

34. *Study for the Group of the Sick* in the "Hundred Guilder Print". About 1639-40. Pen and bistre, wash, white body-colour. Berlin, Kupferstichkabinett.

35. *The Death of Jacob.* About 1640-2. Pen and brush in bistre, wash, touches with white body-colour. Montreal, Museum of Fine Arts.

36. *View of London with Old St. Paul's, seen from the North.* About 1640. Pen and bistre, wash, white body-colour. Berlin, Kupferstichkabinett.

37. *Cottages before a Stormy Sky in Sunlight.* About 1641. Pen and washes in bistre and Indian ink. Vienna, Albertina.

38. *Isaac blessing Jacob*. About 1640-2. Pen, brush and wash in bistre, touches in Indian ink. Formerly Vienna, Oscar Bondi.

39. *The Good Samaritan.* About 1641-3. Pen and wash in bistre, corrected with white body-colour. Rotterdam, Museum Boymans/Van Beuningen.

40. *The Holy Family in the Carpenter's Workshop.* About 1640-2. Pen and bistre, washes in bistre and Indian ink. London, British Museum.

41. *The Star of the Kings.* About 1641-2. Pen and bistre, wash. London, British Museum.

42. *The Incredulity of St. Thomas.* About 1640-2. Pen and brush in bistre. Paris, Georges Renand.

43. *The Brethren of Joseph requesting Benjamin from their Father.* About 1643. Pen and bistre. Amsterdam, Rijksprentenkabinet.

44 *David taking Leave of Jonathan*. About 1642-4. Pen and wash in bistre. Paris, Louvre.

45. *Cottage near the Entrance to a Wood*. 1644. Pen and bistre, wash, some black and red chalk. New York, Robert Lehman Collection.

46. *The Holy Family in the Carpenter's Workshop*. About 1645. Pen and bistre. Bayonne, Musée, Collection L. Bonnat.

47. *The Angel at the open Tomb of Christ.* About 1647-8.
Pen and bistre, corrections in white body-colour.
Barnsley Park, Cirencester, Lord Faringdon.

48. *Male Nude standing, resting his left Arm on a Cushion*. About 1646. Pen and wash in bistre. Vienna, Albertina.

49. *Study for the Figure of Susanna.* About 1647. Black chalk. Berlin, Kupferstichkabinett.

50. *Jan Six standing by a Window, reading.* About 1647. Black chalk. Amsterdam, Six Collection.

51. *The Sacrifice of Iphigenia.* About 1647. Pen and bistre, with some white body-colour. Paris, A. Normand.

52. *The Holy Family in the Carpenter's Workshop.* About 1648-9. Pen and bistre. Rotterdam, Museum Boymans/Van Beuningen.

53. *Jael and Sisera*. About 1648-9. Pen and bistre. Oxford, Ashmolean Museum.

54. *The Western Gate at Rhenen.* About 1647-8. Pen and bistre, wash. Haarlem, Teyler Museum.

55. *View over the Amstel from the Blauwbrug in Amsterdam.* About 1648-50. Pen and wash on vellum. Amsterdam, Rijksprentenkabinet.

56. The Soldiers gambling for Christ's Garment under the Cross. About 1650. Reed-pen and bistre.
Ottawa, National Gallery of Canada.

57. Seated Man resting his Chin on his right Hand. About 1650-1. Black chalk.
Stephan von Kuffner Collection, formerly Vienna.

58. Old Man seated by a Fireplace, warming his Hands. About 1650. Pen and bistre. London, Colnaghi & Co. (1958).

59. *The Good Samaritan attending to the Wounded Man.* About 1650. Pen and bistre. Barnsley Park, Cirencester, Lord Faringdon.

60. *The Holy Family*. About 1651. Reed-pen and bistre. Berlin, Kupferstichkabinett.

61. *Christ healing a Leper.* About 1652. Reed-pen and bistre, wash, rubbed with the finger, white body-colour. Berlin, Kupferstichkabinett.

62. *The Holy Family departing for Egypt.* About 1652. Reed-pen and bistre, slightly washed, white body-colour. Berlin, Kupferstichkabinett.

63. *St. Jerome reading, in an Italian Landscape.* About 1652. Reed-pen and wash. Hamburg, Kunsthalle.

64. *Homer reciting Verses.* 1652. Reed-pen and bistre. Amsterdam, Six Collection.

65. *Lion resting*. About 1651-2. Pen and brush in bistre, on slightly washed paper. Paris, Louvre.

66. *Trees surrounding a Garden-Door forming the Entrance to an Estate. About 1652. Pen and washes in bistre (enlarged). Hamburg, Kunsthalle.*

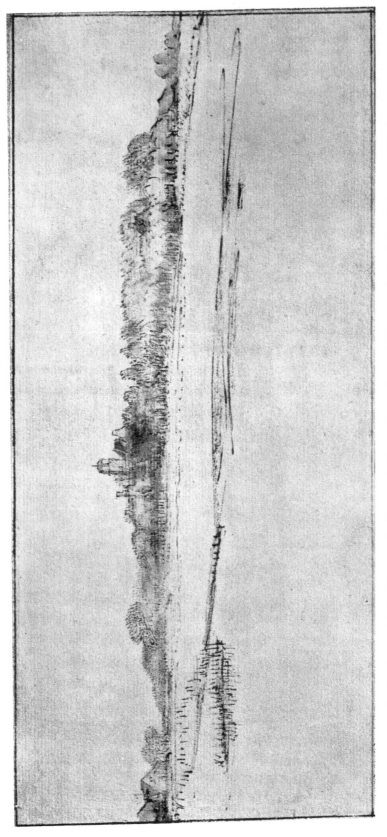

67. *Landscape with the "Huys met het Toorentje."* About 1651-2. Pen and bistre, wash. Basel, Dr. Robert von Hirsch.

68. *View over Het Ij with Sailing Boats at Anchor.* About 1652. Black chalk. Vienna, Albertina.

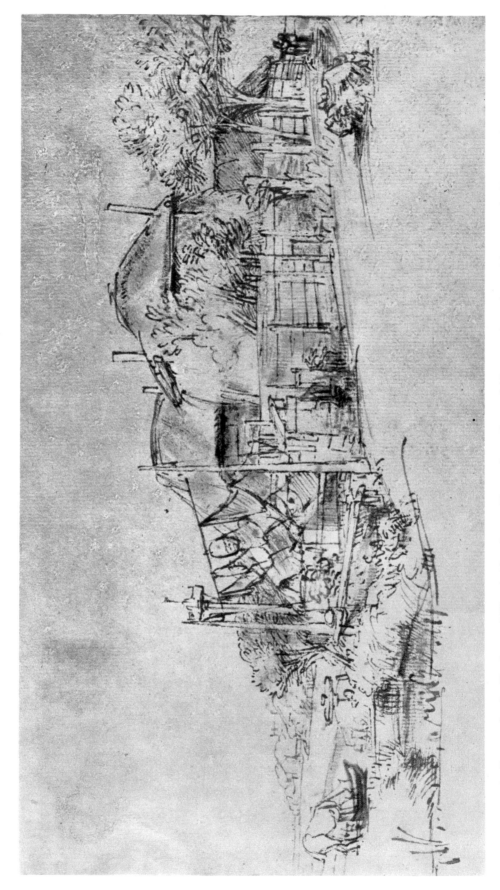

69. *Farmstead with a Hay Barn and Weirs beside a Stream.* About 1652-3. Pen and bistre, wash, on brownish paper. The Hague, F. Lugt.

70. *Windmill on a Bulwark of Amsterdam*. About 1654. Reed-pen and bistre, wash. The Hague, F. Lugt.

71. *River with Trees on its Embankment at Dusk.* About 1654-5. Pen and bistre. Paris, Louvre.

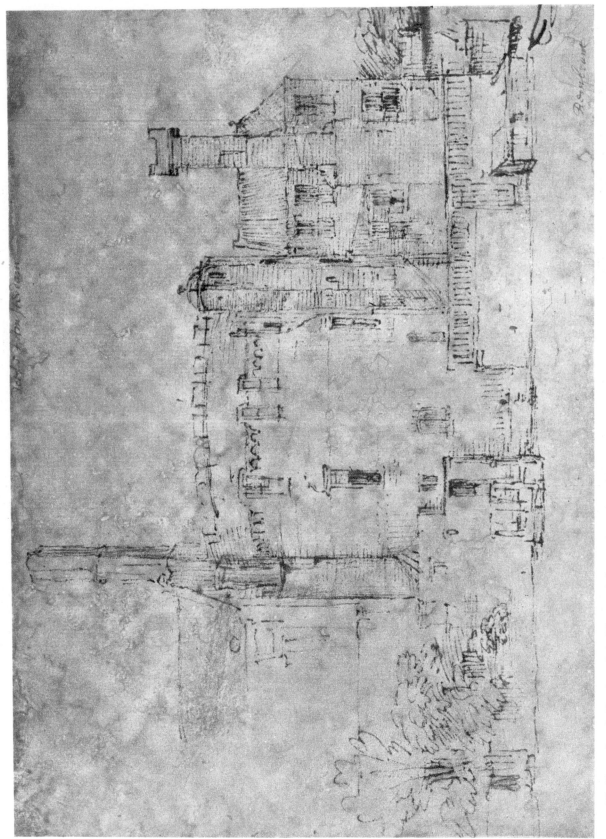

72. *The Tower Swijght-Utrecht and the Kloveniersdoelen in Amsterdam.* About 1654-5. Reed-pen and bistre, on brownish paper. Amsterdam, A. Boerlage-Koenigs.

73. *The Dismissal of Hagar.* About 1652-3. Pen and bistre. Amsterdam, Rijksprentenkabinet.

74. *Christ among the Doctors.* About 1653-4. Reed-pen and bistre. Stockholm, Nationalmuseum.

75. *The Prophet Elijah by the Brook Cherith. About 1654-5.* Reed-pen and bistre, wash, some white body-colour. Berlin, Kupferstichkabinett.

76. *Nathan admonishing David.* About 1654-5. Reed-pen and bistre, wash. Berlin, Kupferstichkabinett.

77. *Wide Landscape with a Tree and a Windmill amidst Houses beside a Canal in the middle distance. About 1654-5. Reed-pen and wash in bistre. Vienna, Albertina.*

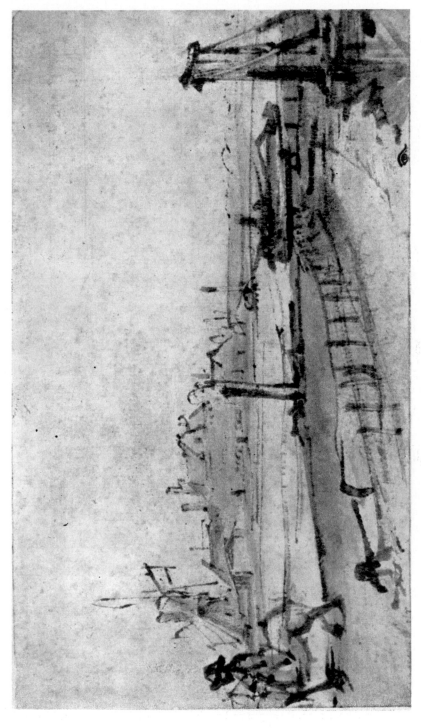

78. *"Het Molentje", seen from the Amsteldijk; a Barge is being towed by a Man on Horseback.* About 1655. Pen and bistre, wash. Oxford, Ashmolean Museum.

L'ange quitte Manüé et sa femme, et s'éleve au milieu de la flame qu'il auoit excitée 1807. 79

79. *Manoah's Offering*. About 1655. Reed-pen and wash in Indian ink. Stockholm, Nationalmuseum.

80. *Noli me tangere*. About 1655-6. Pen and bistre. The Hague, F. Lugt.

gerekent door Rembrant van Rhijn naer sijn selver...

81. *Self-Portrait in Studio Attire, full-length*. About 1655-6. Pen and bistre, on brownish paper.
Amsterdam, Rembrandt-Huis.

82. *Young Woman seated in an Arm-Chair*. About 1655-6. Reed-pen and wash in blackish-brown bistre. London, British Museum.

83. *Seated Female Nude wearing a Japanese Straw Hat.* About 1654-6. Pen and olive grey brown bistre, wash
with Indian ink. London, Victoria and Albert Museum.

84. *Boy drawing at a Desk (probably Titus)*. About 1655-6. Pen, bistre and brush, rubbed with the finger. Dresden, Kupferstichkabinett.

85. *Woman looking out of a Window.* About 1655-6. Pen and brush in bistre. Paris, Louvre.

86. *A Girl sleeping; Study after Hendrickje*. About 1655-6. Brush and bistre, wash. London, British Museum.

87. *An Indian Prince, probably Emperor Jahangir as a Young Man.* About 1654-6. Pen and brush in bistre, wash, on Japanese paper. Copy after an Indian miniature. Vienna, Albertina.

88. *Shah Jahan with a Falcon, on Horseback.* About 1654-6. Pen and bistre, slightly touched with red chalk wash, on Japanese paper. Copy after an Indian miniature. Paris, Louvre.

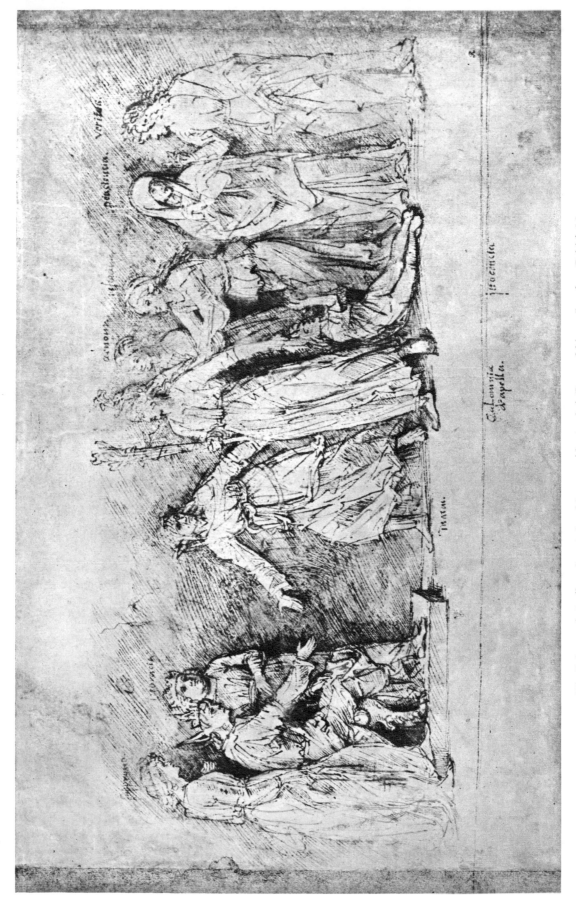

89. *The Calumny of Apelles, after Andrea Mantegna.* About 1656. Pen and bistre. London, British Museum.

90. *Christ in the Storm on the Sea of Galilee;* in the upper right corner, *Bust of a frightened Apostle.* About 1654-5. Pen and bistre. Dresden, Kupferstichkabinett.

91. *The Holy Maries at the Sepulchre.* About 1656. Pen and bistre, wash. Rotterdam, Museum Boymans/Van Beuningen.

92. *The Incredulity of St. Thomas.* About 1656. Pen and bistre, corrections with white body-colour. Paris, Louvre.

93. *Female Nude with her Head bent forward, asleep. About 1657-8. Pen and brush in bistre, some oxidized white. Amsterdam, Rijksprentenkabinet.*

94. *Cottages beneath high Trees in bright Sunlight.* About 1657–8. Pen and brush in bistre, wash. Berlin, Kupferstichkabinett.

95. *The Return of the Prodigal Son.* About 1658-9. Pen and bistre. Vienna, Albertina.

96. *The Vision of St. Peter.* About 1658-9. Pen and bistre. Munich, Graphische Sammlung.

E.F.

97. *Christ healing a Sick Woman.* About 1659-60. Pen and bistre, wash, white body-colour. The Hague, F. Lugt.

98. *The Arrest of Christ.* About 1659-60. Pen and bistre, wash. Stockholm, Nationalmuseum.

99. *St. Martin and the Beggar.* About 1660. Pen and bistre, slightly washed. Besançon, Musée Communal.

100. *The Conspiracy of Julius Civilis*. About 1660-1. Pen and bistre, wash, some white body-colour.
Munich, Graphische Sammlung.

101. *Female Nude with a long Veil seated on a Chair before a Curtain*. About 1661. Pen and wash in bistre,
some red and white chalk. Rotterdam, Museum Boymans/Van Beuningen.

102. *The standing Syndic.* About 1662. Pen, brush and bistre, wash, white body-colour.
Rotterdam, Museum Boymans/Van Beuningen.

103. *St. Peter at the Death-Bed of Tabitha*. About 1662-5. Pen and bistre. Dresden, Kupferstichkabinett.

104. *Diana and Actaeon*, after Antonio Tempesta. About 1662-5. Pen and bistre, wash, white body-colour. Dresden, Kupferstichkabinett.

105. *The Presentation in the Temple.* 1661.
Pen and brush in bistre, white body-colour.
The Hague, Royal Library.

CATALOGUE

BIBLIOGRAPHY
(INCLUDING ABBREVIATIONS)
OF THE MAIN LITERATURE
QUOTED IN THE TEXT

B. – A. Bartsch, Catalogue raisonné de toutes les estampes qui forment l'œuvre de Rembrandt . . . Vienne 1797.

Benesch – Otto Benesch, The Drawings of Rembrandt (A Critical and Chronological Catalogue). Vols. I–VI. London 1954–57.

Bredius – A. Bredius, The Paintings of Rembrandt, Vienna–London 1937; Second Edition, London–New York n.d.

HdG, see C. Hofstede de Groot.

Hind – A. M. Hind, A Catalogue of Rembrandt's Etchings. Vols. 1, 2. London 1923.

C. Hofstede de Groot, Die Handzeichnungen Rembrandts. Haarlem 1906.

Lugt – F. Lugt, Les Marques des Collections de Dessins et d'Estampes, Amsterdam 1921; Supplément, The Hague, 1956.

Münz – Ludwig Münz, Rembrandt's Etchings (A Critical Catalogue), Vols. I, II. London 1952.

Valentiner – Wilhelm R. Valentiner, Rembrandt. Des Meisters Handzeichnungen. Vols. 1, 2. Klassiker der Kunst 31, 32, Stuttgart, Berlin.

A systematic bibliography of the literature on Rembrandt will be found in the appendix to O. Benesch, Rembrandt, Werk und Forschung, Wien 1935, and in H. van Hall, Repertorium voor de Geschiedenis der Nederlandsche Schilder- en Graveer Kunst I, II, s'Gravenhage, 1935, 1949.

CATALOGUE

1. THE RAISING OF THE CROSS

About 1627–8. Black chalk. 193 × 148 mm.
Rotterdam, Museum Boymans.
Inscribed by a later hand: Rembrant.
HdG 1362; Benesch 6 recto.

Important specimen of a compositional drawing of Rembrandt's early period. It recasts an idea which harks back to Dürer and Altdorfer, and was also taken up by Rubens in his altar-piece in the Cathedral of Antwerp. Whereas Rubens emphasizes the physical impact of the dramatic diagonal composition, Rembrandt lends it a flaming and spiritualized expression.

2. OLD MAN WITH A BOOK, SEATED IN PROFILE TO RIGHT, FULL-LENGTH

Red and black chalk, heightened with white. 295 × 210 mm.
Berlin, Kupferstichkabinett.
HdG 112; Benesch 7.

Careful drawing after the model, embodying the thorough study of nature, as practised by the followers of Caravaggio in Utrecht and Amsterdam. Used for the figure of one of the *Two Philosophers in Discussion* (fig. 3), a painting of 1628 in the National Gallery of Victoria, Melbourne (Bredius 423).

3. OLD MAN WITH HIS ARMS EXTENDED

About 1629. Black chalk. 254 × 190 mm.
Dresden, Kupferstichkabinett.
HdG 233; Benesch 12.

Expressive momentary study after an old man, perhaps a beggar who inspired the figure of St. Peter in Rembrandt's early etching *St. Peter and St. John healing the Paralysed at the Gate of the Temple*, fig. 4 (B. 95, Hind 5, Münz 188).

4. THE ENTOMBMENT OF CHRIST

Dated 1630. Red chalk, heightened with white. 280 × 203 mm.
London, British Museum.
HdG 891; Benesch 17.

This composition was originally planned by Rembrandt as a *Raising of Lazarus* whose soaring and lofty aspect foreshadows the etching B. 72, Hind 198, Münz 214. As such, the composition influenced a painting (Hans Schneider, *Jan Lievens*, No. 31) and an etching by Jan Lievens (B. 3), representing the same subject. By inserting the group of men with the body of Christ, Rembrandt changed the composition to its present form.

5. OLD MAN WITH CLASPED HANDS, SEATED IN AN ARM-CHAIR, FULL-LENGTH

About 1631. Red and black chalk. 226 × 157 mm.
Berlin, Kupferstichkabinett.
Benesch 41.

In 1630–31 Rembrandt made a series of red chalk drawings after one or several models of old men whom he used as figures of patriarchs or apostles in paintings and etchings. The stroke of the red chalk, compared with No. 2, has achieved here greater fluidity and freedom, hence the increased expressiveness in the rendering of mood and light. The figure was used by Rembrandt for the painting of 1633, *A Scholar seated in an Interior* (Bredius 431), representing with all probability Tobit and Anna. The lightly sketched background already indicates that of the painting.

6. YOUNG WOMAN AT HER TOILET

About 1632–4. Pen and bistre, washes in bistre and Indian ink. 238 × 184 mm.
Vienna, Albertina.
HdG 1453; Benesch 395.

A brilliant study from nature, characteristic of Rembrandt's keen observation during the first years of his stay in Amsterdam. The sitter has usually been considered to be Saskia, which would imply that the drawing was done not earlier than in 1634. The same subject, however, appears transformed into a Biblical scene in the painting of 1632

Bathsheba at her Toilet in the National Gallery of Canada, Ottawa (Bredius 494). Thus the drawing may have been done before the painting, in which case it would represent Rembrandt's sister Lisbeth.

7. PORTRAIT OF SASKIA STANDING, holding a Flower (?) in her right Hand, full-length.

About 1633. Pen and brush in bistre. 223 × 151 mm.
London, Hugh N. Squire.

About 1633 Rembrandt drew numerous studies after nature – people whom he observed in the street, orientals in magnificent attires and the persons he saw in his own house. Saskia was also drawn frequently in this way, not as a portrait study proper but engaged in some domestic occupation; e.g. in Benesch 217 (Bremen, Print Room) she seems to be selecting jewellery from a drawer of her dressing table in order to adorn herself.

The present drawing, hitherto unpublished, is very close in style and expression to the one in Bremen, but here the study from nature rises to a true portrait, showing Saskia, full-length, in rich dress as the master liked to paint her. In this way originated one of the most magnificent early portraits of Rembrandt. Rembrandt enhanced the colourful plasticity of the figure by surrounding her with vigorous touches of the brush as if it were by a mantle.

This portrait study was recognized as such by A. E. Popham and J. Byam Shaw. I am indebted to Mr. Hugh N. Squire for granting permission to publish it.

8. PORTRAIT OF SASKIA IN A STRAW HAT

Dated 1633. Silver-point on white prepared vellum. 185 × 107 mm.
Berlin, Kupferstichkabinett.
HdG 99; Benesch 427.

Dutch inscription in the artist's hand. Translation: This is drawn after my wife, when she was 21 years old, the third day after our betrothal – the 8th of June 1633. A very personal document of the artist's life and at the same time a drawing of highest artistic quality. It was a reminder to the artist of his betrothal. The marriage took place in the little country-church of the parish of St. Anne at Het Bilt.

9. PORTRAIT OF A GENTLEMAN IN AN ARM-CHAIR, SEEN THROUGH A WINDOW-FRAME

Signed and dated: Rembrandt f. 1634. Red and black chalk, pen and wash, on vellum. 373 × 272 mm.
New York, Mrs. Charles S. Payson.
HdG 1063, Benesch 433.

This is the only portrait drawing by Rembrandt known so far which was apparently commissioned as a finished work of art in its own right. It is remarkable for the masterly modelling of the figure in soft light, melting away all harsh contrasts and thus creating delicious gradations and transitions. The way of representing the sitter as if he were placed in a different room from the spectator and communicating with the latter through a window was repeatedly adopted by Rembrandt, also in painted portraits. It increased the expression of intimacy and personal relation between model and spectator, particularly when enhanced as here by the contrast of a dark framing and an area of light beyond. Bredius and Valentiner tentatively identified the sitter as Maurits Huygens, the brother of Rembrandt's friend and Maecenas Constantijn Huygens.

10. THE RAISING OF THE DAUGHTER OF JAIRUS

About 1632–3. Pen and bistre. 188 × 240 mm.
Formerly Rotterdam, F. Koenigs Collection.
Benesch 61.

Besides numerous portrait commissions for the wealthy burghers of Amsterdam which Rembrandt had to fulfil during the first years of his stay in the city, he devoted himself eagerly to inventing biblical compositions which he usually drew with a sharp quill-pen. They prove the great expressiveness and liveliness of his inner vision. The role of every figure is most eloquently represented: Christ speaking the consoling words to the mourners "The maid is not dead but sleepeth" (St. Matthew ix, 24) and the physician bent over the deceased trying to catch a faint breath. The latter motive foreshadows the famous etching *The Death of the Virgin* (B. 99, Hind 161, Münz 208) of 1639, done by Rembrandt more than half a decade later.

11. JESUS AND HIS DISCIPLES

Signed and dated: Rembrandt. f: 1634. Black and red chalk, pen and bistre, washes in different tones, heightenings in gouache; the disciple in the middle is drawn on a separate piece of paper, which was superimposed by the artist himself. 355 × 476 mm.
Haarlem, Teyler Museum.
HdG 1319; Benesch 89.

This important drawing of considerable size is closely related in compositional features to the painting of the same year *The Incredulity of St. Thomas*, Leningrad, Hermitage (Bredius 552). It might be regarded as the preparation for a painting, but it may just as well be a work of art in its own right. The elaborate signature and dating speak for the latter possibility. The type of composition proves the importance which Caravaggio's contrast of dark and light gained for Rembrandt. The light used by Rembrandt on such occasions is of supernatural origin. It emanates here from the figure of Christ. In this respect Rembrandt differs from Caravaggio and approaches the principle of light adopted by Tintoretto.

12. THE NAUGHTY BOY

About 1635. Pen and bistre, wash, white body-colour, some black chalk; inscribed by a later hand: Rembrant. 206 × 143 mm.
Berlin, Kupferstichkabinett.
HdG 140; Benesch 401.

Rembrandt was a keen observer of everyday life in the street and at home. He jotted down his impressions in vivacious sketches sparkling with life, movement and psychical tension. A collection of numerous sketches of this kind was sold at the sale of Rembrandt's property under the title *Vrouwenleven* (Life of Women). To this category of drawings the present masterly example also belongs. An unruly boy is carried away by

his mother from his laughing playmates. The grandmother opens the hatch-door of the house and administers serious admonitions which make no impression on the furiously struggling child. Most of Rembrandt's free inventions were occasioned by impressions of real life and this drawing too led to a mythological painting: *Ganymede carried away by the Eagle of Zeus* (Dresden, Gemäldegalerie, 1635, Bredius 471).

13. ABRAHAM'S SACRIFICE

Signed: Rembrandt. Red and black chalk, wash in Indian ink, heightened with white, on greenish yellow paper. 194 × 146 mm.
London, British Museum.
HdG 866; Benesch 90.

This drawing is a preparatory sketch for the painting of 1635 in the Hermitage, Leningrad (Bredius 498), fig. 5. We learn from this example how Rembrandt continuously remoulded his compositional inventions through his creative imagination. The painting as finally executed differs considerably from the drawing: the Angel rushes in from the left whereas in the drawing he suddenly emerges from the background behind Abraham. The Caravaggiesque weight is increased in the painting because the frame is drawn closer around the figures. The drawing was used with fewer changes by a pupil in a painting in the Pinakothek, Munich (dG 8) which Rembrandt corrected himself.

14. THE LAST SUPPER, after Leonardo da Vinci

Signed and dated: Rembrandt f. 1635. Pen and bistre, wash, white body-colour; a 70 mm. strip of paper added on the right; the left portion of the paper is squared out. 128 × 385 mm.
Berlin, Kupferstichkabinett.
HdG 65; Benesch 445.

During 1635 Rembrandt occupied himself intensely with Leonardo's greatest work. He copied it after a mediocre print by one of Leonardo's contemporaries which Hind attributed to the Master of the Sforza Book of Hours. The first outcome of these studies was a red chalk drawing in the Robert Lehman Collection, New York (formerly

Dresden, Benesch 443). Gradually Rembrandt imbued himself with the idea of the work so that in the present drawing he was able to alter the composition considerably with the result that he approached more closely the spirit of the original which he had never seen. Rembrandt hardly intended to use the drawing for a painting so that the squaring out must be attributed to a later hand which numbered the horizontal sections. The paper has been somewhat cut down as the incomplete sketches of heads on the right of the upper margin indicate.

The idea of this great composition of the Renaissance pursued Rembrandt down to his most monumental composition, the *Conspiracy of Julius Civilis*, Stockholm, Nationalmuseum (Bredius 482), see fig. 9.

15. CHRIST CARRYING THE CROSS

About 1635. Pen and bistre, wash; inscribed by a later hand: Rembrant. 145 × 260 mm.
Berlin, Kupferstichkabinett.
HdG 71; Benesch 97.

Christ breaks down under His burden. Veronica faints overpowered by grief. St. John and the Holy Women hasten to her aid. The breathless dynamism approaches in expressive grandeur the copy after Leonardo da Vinci, No. 14. The shadowy figure of the soldier on the left increases the spatial tension of the composition.

16. STUDY FOR THE *Great Jewish Bride*

Pen and Indian ink, wash. 232 × 182 mm.
Stockholm, Nationalmuseum.
HdG 1569; Benesch 292.

Preparatory drawing for the etching of 1635, *The Great Jewish Bride* (B. 340, Hind 127, Münz 90). The subject of the etching is still obscure. W. R. Valentiner (Zeitschrift für Bildende Kunst, 1925–6, p. 270) suggested that it represented an actress with the text of her rôle in her hand. The representation of a biblical Sibyl is perhaps more likely. This drawing, very vigorous in its brilliant effect of chiaroscuro, gives a picturesque outline of the idea of the finished etching, realized afterwards by Rembrandt only in part (the figure cut at her knees).

17. ACTOR ON THE STAGE WITH A PARROT ON HIS RIGHT SHOULDER, STANDING IN FRONT OF THE CURTAIN; BELOW, A SPECTATOR CLAPPING

About 1635. Pen and bistre. 174 × 127 mm.
Vienna, Albertina (Inv. 32765).

About 1635, Rembrandt made a series of sketches after actors on the stage. They render momentary impressions, buoyant and unsurpassable in their art of quick characterization. The present drawing, hitherto unpublished, represents one of the comic characters of the cast. See also the note to No. 16.

18. SASKIA ASLEEP IN BED

About 1635. Pen and brush in bistre; inscribed by a later hand: Renbrant. 137 × 203 mm.
Oxford, Ashmolean Museum.
Benesch Addenda 4.

Rembrandt made many drawings of Saskia in bed during her confinements or her frequent illnesses. The present drawing was probably done on the same occasion as Benesch 281 (formerly J. P. Heseltine). The figure was drawn with the quill-pen and afterwards rounded off with brilliant touches of the brush which complete the pillows, indicate the bed curtain and lend light and colourful life to the motive.

19. A BRAWL OF PEASANTS IN AN INN

About 1637. Pen and bistre, wash. 160 × 220 mm.
Montpellier, Musée Fabre.
HdG 583; Benesch Addenda A 2.

The subject-matter was repeatedly treated by Bruegel, Rubens and Brouwer. The dynamic vigour of such creations by the Flemish masters seems to have impressed Rembrandt in the 1630's when he dealt with similar problems of momentary movement. The present invention is a reflection of it. Comparisons with similar scenes of movement of the middle of the 1630's (e.g. Nos. 14, 15) prove the undoubted authenticity of the present drawing although its subject does not occur in Rembrandt's œuvre elsewhere.

20. SELF-PORTRAIT IN CLOAK AND LARGE BARETT, BUST

About 1636. Pen and wash, in bistre and Indian ink. 145 × 121 mm.
Formerly New York, Dr. A. Hamilton Rice.
Benesch 434.

We are used to seeing Rembrandt in his self-representations from the early period in radiant optimism or self-conscious superiority. The mood of deep depression which speaks eloquently from this portrait has led scholars to date it very late: in the time of his deepest humiliation. However, the technique of drawing and graphic evidence prove the contrary. Besides, Rembrandt's features are young and lean and not as square and stout as in his late self-portraits. Clouds may have overshadowed this great and tragic spirit in all periods of his life, without detriment to the basic optimism and religious confidence of his soul.

21. SASKIA CARRYING RUMBARTUS (?) DOWN STAIRS

About 1636. Pen and bistre, wash. 185 × 133 mm.
New York, Pierpont Morgan Library.
Benesch 313; Wilhelm R. Valentiner, Zur Kunstgeschichte des Auslandes, XXIX, p. 29.

Rumbartus, Rembrandt's and Saskia's eldest son was baptized on December 15, 1635. Miss I. H. van Eeghen has published an entry in the register of funerals of the Zuiderkerk stating that Rembrandt had buried one of his children on February 15, 1636 (Jaarboek Amstelodamum 43, October 1956, pp. 144 ff.) She assumes that this entry which mentions no name may concern Rumbartus. If Miss Van Eeghen's assumption should be correct, the boy identified with Rumbartus in such portraits as for instance Benesch 313a recto (Amsterdam, Rembrandt-Huis) could not be Rumbartus.

22. FARM-HOUSE AMID A COPSE

About 1636. Pen and bistre, wash. 138 × 244 mm.
Vienna, Bibliothek der Akademie der Bildenden Künste.
Benesch 471.

The drawing reveals in its simplicity the striking greatness and astounding modernity of Rembrandt's artistic vision. Such drawings Rembrandt jotted down on the sheets of sketch-books when strolling through the fields on extensive walks around Amsterdam.

23. FARM-HOUSE IN SUNLIGHT

About 1636. Pen and wash; inscribed by a later hand: Rembrant. 165 × 223 mm.
Budapest, Museum of Fine Arts.
HdG 1393; Benesch 463.

Whereas in landscape painting Rembrandt mostly created heroic and pathetic compositions, in drawing he was engrossed with the study of nature seen in reality. Two magnificent views of this farm-house are preserved: the present one and a close-up of the little pantry in front of the gable covered by a climbing plant (Benesch 464, also in Budapest).

24. ST. JOHN THE BAPTIST PREACHING

About 1637. Quill-pen (perhaps also reed-pen) and wash in bistre. 194 × 277 mm.
Private Collection.
Benesch Addenda 10.

Preparatory drawing for the painting in Berlin, Staatliche Gemäldesammlungen (Bredius 555), fig. 6. This composition, rich in many eloquent figures and groups, was executed by Rembrandt in monochrome about 1637. It gains particular interest through the circumstance that the panel was enlarged by Rembrandt when he began working on it, and at least four drawings preparatory for it are known to us. Besides the present drawing giving a cursory outline of the entire composition, there exist three sheets of sketches showing different types and groups of figures among the Baptist's audience (Benesch 140, 141, 142). All four drawings were meant as preparations for the painting and to assist its progress. See also the note to the following drawing.

25. STUDIES FOR GROUPS AND FIGURES
in the Painting in Berlin, *St. John the Baptist preaching* (Bredius 555).

About 1637. Pen and bistre. 167 × 196 mm.
Berlin, Kupferstichkabinett.
HdG 158, Benesch 141.

This brilliant sheet of sketches is preparatory mainly for the group of Doctors in the centre foreground of the painting which was repeated at least six times. Furthermore, single figures have been tried out. Rembrandt did not sketch here after nature but drew from the rich fund of his visual experience which enabled him to realize his visions and inventions at any given moment.

26. SUSANNA AND THE TWO ELDERS

About 1637. Red chalk. Signed: R f. 235 × 364 mm.
Berlin, Kupferstichkabinett.
HdG 45, Benesch 448.

Free copy after a painting of Pieter Lastman in Berlin, Staatliche Gemäldesammlungen, Valentiner 632A. It confirms the interest which Rembrandt as a highly developed artist still took in the work of his master. The changes purport improvements in the design according to Rembrandt's own artistic vision. The emphasis on angular and edged forms differs from the smooth and doughy modelling of Lastman's. On the reverse, some notes by Rembrandt concerning paintings by himself of 1635 and paintings by his pupils F. Bol and L. C. van Beyeren.

From 1637 onward, this subject occupied Rembrandt for almost two decades both in drawing and painting.

27. AN ELEPHANT

Signed and dated: Rembrandt ft. 1637. Black chalk. 233 × 356 mm.
Vienna, Albertina.
HdG 1469; Benesch 457 and vol. VI, p. 431, Addenda.

This is the most masterly animal study of Rembrandt's early period. There exist two more studies of elephants (Benesch 458, Albertina; Benesch 459, British Museum) and furthermore a counter-proof after a lost one (Benesch 460, The Pierpont Morgan Library). Animals appear in the backgrounds of works of Rembrandt about that time, particularly in representations of biblical subjects (e.g. the etching *Adam and Eve* of 1638, B. 28, Hind 159, Münz 177).

28. THE GOOD SAMARITAN ATTENDING TO THE WOUNDED MAN

About 1637. Pen and bistre. 133 × 138 mm. Barnsley Park, Cirencester, Lord Faringdon.

This hitherto unpublished drawing is the earliest treatment of the subject-matter by Rembrandt so far known. The figure group is remarkable because of its violent foreshortening in space, characteristic of Rembrandt's dramatic style in the 1630's. A comparison with a drawing of the same subject in Berlin, dated 1644 (Benesch 556), is revealing. The head of the wounded man was sketched in three different versions, following each other. There exists in the same collection a pupil's copy after a somewhat different version of the same composition by Rembrandt, the whereabouts of which are unknown. I am indebted to Lord Faringdon for granting permission to publish the present drawing and also Nos. 47, 59, in his collection.

29. TWO NEGRO DRUMMERS MOUNTED ON MULES

About 1637-8. Pen and wash in bistre, coloured with red chalk and yellow watercolour, heightened with white, some oil colour. 229 × 171 mm.
London, British Museum.
HdG 924; Benesch 365.

Begun with the pen and washed with bistre afterwards. Some parts of the garment of the drummer in front and the cover of his drum were filled in with yellow watercolour. The red chalk of collars and parasol was worked into the washed paper while it was still wet. The white spaces of the bridle, the drums and the shoes were filled in with red chalk. The face of the drummer in front seems to be modelled with the brush dipped in some oil colour.

J. Qu. van Regteren Altena suggested that Rembrandt made the drawing in February 1638 when observing the pageant of a tournament from the house of Constantijn Huygens in the Hague. To the same group belong three more drawings (Benesch 366-368). Rembrandt's keen interest in the colourful performance is proved by the use of different media in varying colours and shades. The mat and dark hue of the drummer in front is admirably rendered.

30. FEMALE NUDE WITH A SNAKE (PROBABLY CLEOPATRA)

About 1637. Red chalk. 245 × 140 mm.
London, Villiers David.
Benesch 137.

A realistic study after the living model to which a mythological meaning has been given by the attribute of a snake. Hygieia and Cleopatra have been suggested. The same truth to life is characteristic of the representation of Eve in the etching of 1638 (B. 28, Hind 159, Münz 177).

31. PORTRAIT OF TITIA VAN UYLENBURCH (1605–1641)

Inscribed and dated by the artist: Tijtsya van Ulenburch 1639; by a later hand: Rhimbrand. Pen and bistre. 178 × 146 mm.
Stockholm, Nationalmuseum.
HdG 1567; Benesch 441.

One of the most intimate portrait studies of Rembrandt's family circle. Titia, an elder sister of Saskia, was married to François Copal, Commissioner of Vlissingen. They were godparents of Rembrandt's children.

32. SASKIA'S LYING-IN ROOM

About 1639. Pen and bistre, washes in bistre and Indian ink, heightened with white. 143 × 176 mm.
The Hague, F. Lugt.
W. R. Valentiner, Aus Rembrandts Häuslichkeit, Jahrbuch für Kunstwissenschaft I (1923), Pl. 114, p. 279. – Benesch 426.

One of the most beautiful and accomplished examples of Rembrandt's representation of his domestic surroundings. Valentiner has established that Saskia's bedroom in the house in the Jodenbreestraat is represented here. The fire-place at the left is the same which Rembrandt sketched in a much later drawing (Benesch 1156) showing Women sewing by lamplight. The house, acquired by Rembrandt in 1639, still exists today.

33. PORTRAIT OF BALDASSARE CASTIGLIONE, after Raphael

Dated 1639. Pen and bistre, some white body-colour. 163 × 207 mm.
Vienna, Albertina.
HdG 1430; Benesch 451.

Dutch inscription in the artist's hand. Translation: The Count Balthasar Castiglione by Raphael/ sold for 3500 guilders/ the whole cargo of Lucas van Nuffeelen fetched/ fl. 59456. Anno 1639.
Drawing after Raphael's painting (about 1519), Paris, Louvre. Rembrandt was an ardent art collector. He had a high reputation as a connoisseur among dealers and collectors, being a well-known figure at Amsterdam sales. The present sketch was made at an auction, arranged by the dealer Lucas van Uffelen, on April 9, 1639. The rough and brilliant sketch is an excellent example of how Rembrandt transformed classical models into his own idiom, interpreting their greatness of form through strength of accent.

34. STUDY (IN REVERSE) FOR THE GROUP OF THE SICK in the *Hundred Guilder Print* (B. 74, Hind 236, Münz 217).

About 1639–40. Pen and bistre, wash, white body-colour. 144 × 185 mm.
Berlin, Kupferstichkabinett.
HdG 56; Benesch 188.

The *Hundred Guilder Print* is perhaps the chief work of Rembrandt's graphic art, at least as to length of time consumed for creating it. It is also Rembrandt's most popular print, as the *Night Watch* is his most popular painting. Both were created in the 1640's. That Rembrandt began with the first drawings for this elaborate etching already at the end of the 1630's is proved by the present sketch. The parapet, which in the etching supports Christ's left arm, is indicated here by the edge of a wall to the right of the woman praying. The shadow which her raised hands throw on it falls on Christ's garment in the etching.

35. THE DEATH OF JACOB

About 1640–42. Pen and brush in bistre, wash, touches with white body-colour. 231 × 353 mm.
Montreal, Canada, Museum of Fine Arts (Art Association of Montreal).
Benesch 493 and vol. VI, p. 431, Addenda.
This monumental and dramatic scene is a

further development of the compositional idea of the etching the *Death of the Virgin* (B. 99, Hind 161, Münz 208). Its dramatic impact is in great part due to the masterly handling of the chiaroscuro, which suggests a flood of celestial light penetrating the darkness of the death-chamber. Also related to the etching *The Presentation in the Temple* (B. 49, Hind 162, Münz 210), mainly in its mastery of light.

36. VIEW OF LONDON WITH OLD ST. PAUL'S, SEEN FROM THE NORTH

About 1640. Pen and bistre, wash, white body-colour. 164×318 mm.
Berlin, Kupferstichkabinett.
HdG 170; Benesch 788.

The drawing belongs to a period of Rembrandt's career in which he was very much interested in mediaeval architecture and made several sketches after old English cathedrals. It would be wrong, however, to infer from this a stay of the artist in England. The master used drawn or engraved views as models, as is shown by a drawing of the same subject in the Albertina (Benesch 787) which clings much closer to the (unknown) model. In the present drawing the artist has enlivened a dry view by his power of vision.

37. COTTAGES BEFORE A STORMY SKY IN SUNLIGHT

About 1641. Pen and washes in bistre and Indian ink. 182×245 mm.
Vienna, Albertina.
HdG 1484; Benesch 800.

A storm has passed over the peaceful village and is now moving away to the left while sunlight is flooding the scene. This foreshadows the dramatic light effect of the etching of 1643, *The Three Trees* (B. 212, Hind 205, Münz 152).

38. ISAAC BLESSING JACOB

About 1640–42. Pen, brush and wash in bistre, touches in Indian ink. 186×249 mm.
Formerly Vienna, Oscar Bondi Collection.
Benesch 509.

At this time Rembrandt dealt with the biblical subject represented here in several drawings. The present one is the most monumental and the most important for his future development. A compositional idea is first seen here which was to reach its climax in the painting of 1656 in Cassel, *Jacob blessing the Children of Joseph* (Bredius 525). The large and sure tracing of the lines deviates markedly from the flickering restlessness and reiterations of Rembrandt's linear technique of the 1630's.

39. THE GOOD SAMARITAN: the wounded Man is carried to the Inn.

About 1641–3. Pen and wash in bistre, corrected with white body-colour. 209×310 mm.
Rotterdam, Museum Boymans.
HdG 1350; Benesch 518 b.

Rembrandt had already devoted an etching to the biblical parable in the early 1630's. In the present drawing and in a slightly earlier one in London, British Museum (Benesch 518a) he dealt with the subject-matter in the spirit of Elsheimer's landscapes: in the darkness of the night with rain pouring from clouds on wild forests, the train of the Good Samaritan arrives. Lights flickering in the storm flame up here and there and illuminate the dramatic nucleus of the story: the wounded man lifted from the horse in the centre, the Samaritan paying the inn-keeper at the right. A dog moves animatedly in the right lower corner while spectators look from the windows at the scene.

Rembrandt seems to have intended to paint this composition. The picture, however, was not carried out by him but some years later by an anonymous pupil in the famous painting in the Louvre (Bredius 581).

40. THE HOLY FAMILY IN THE CARPENTER'S WORKSHOP

About 1640–42. Pen and bistre, washes in bistre and Indian ink. 184×246 mm.
London, British Museum.
Benesch 516.

As in the contemporary paintings, a rich scale of washes envelops the holy scene in the quiet poetry of a dusky interior. All the brighter is the gleam of light entering through the window on whose pane a neighbour knocks. This theme together with the oval form of the centre window-pane recurs later in Rembrandt's etched work in various transformations: Faust in his Study (B. 270, Hind 260, Münz 275), The Holy Family of 1654 (B. 63, Hind 275, Münz 229).

41. THE STAR OF THE KINGS

About 1641–2. Pen and bistre, wash; a figure at the right obliterated with wash. Signed: Rembrandt f. 204×323 mm. London, British Museum. HdG 1129; Benesch 736.

The flaming star, the sharp illumination of the figures and the shadows lurking behind them prove that a night scene is represented. The crowd of figures moving in different directions reminds us that Rembrandt worked at that time on the *Night Watch*. The subject was treated once again in an etching several years later (B. 113, Hind 254, Münz 278).

42. THE INCREDULITY OF ST. THOMAS

About 1640–42. Pen and brush in bistre. 184×275 mm. Paris, Georges Renand. Benesch 511a and vol. VI, p. 431, Addenda.

The subtle spell of light achieves a solemn and mysterious effect. The material light of the fire to the left around which the Apostles are sitting is contrasted with the supernatural light emanating from Christ and transfiguring the centre group. The Apostles turn round in silent awe. Mary and the Magdalen are also present. To the left of Christ the paper has been joined together from two sheets. The idea that the Apostles in a locked room sit around a camp fire is not quite appropriate. It may be conjectured that the left half of the drawing was originally intended to represent a Denial of St. Peter.

43. THE BRETHREN OF JOSEPH REQUESTING BENJAMIN FROM THEIR FATHER

About 1643. Pen and bistre. 176×231 mm. Amsterdam, Rijksprentenkabinet. HdG 1160; Benesch 541.

The drawing shows well Rembrandt's capability to deepen the quiet flow of narration in the 1640's. The brethren try to persuade old father Jacob to let Benjamin accompany them to Egypt. The eldest brother, Reuben, is the speaker while the others look at their father waiting tensely to know how he will decide. Benjamin, the object of their discussion, is standing impassively at his father's side. The brother to the left is drawn on a superimposed sheet of paper, a method of correction which in Holland only Rembrandt practised. The left leg of the brother behind Reuben was drawn too long. Rembrandt eliminated this first version with white body-colour.

44. DAVID TAKING LEAVE OF JONATHAN. I Samuel xx.

About 1643–4. Pen and wash in bistre; inscribed by a later hand: Rimbrant 1634. 180×235 mm. Paris, Louvre, L. Bonnat Bequest. HdG 693; Benesch 552.

The friends meet on the bank of a river, which reflects their figures. The rich scenic setting of the biblical event is characteristic of Rembrandt's style in the 1640's when he began to devote himself to the art of landscape on a larger scale.

45. COTTAGE NEAR THE ENTRANCE TO A WOOD

Pen and bistre, wash, some black and red chalk. Signed and dated: Rembrandt f. 1644. New York, Robert Lehman Collection. HdG 1049; Benesch 815.

A drawing after nature in its own right as Rembrandt demonstrated by signing and dating it carefully. The use of all media of drawing familiar to Rembrandt proves that he tried to give to this work some of the pictorial significance which other draughtsmen expressed by the use of water-colours. The same motive occurs in a drawing by Rembrandt's pupil, Lambert Doomer (Louvre; F. Lugt, Inventaire Géneral des Dessins, École Hollandaise I, p. 33, No. 245), which has given rise to the assumption that Doomer made it on a joint trip with his master.

46. THE HOLY FAMILY IN THE CARPENTER'S WORKSHOP

Pen and bistre. 161×158 mm.

Bayonne, Musée, Collection L. Bonnat.
HdG 683; Benesch 567.

This layout for one of Rembrandt's most poetical paintings, dated 1645 (Leningrad, Hermitage, Bredius 570), full of feeling and religious contemplativeness, was destined for the artist's use only. By condensing the flow of his imagination into a few functional and constructive strokes of the pen, Rembrandt achieved that unfailing grasp of his inner vision which he deployed afterwards in the fabulous richness of his luminous palette. In this way he developed also essential elements of his mature style of drawing.

47. THE ANGEL AT THE OPEN TOMB OF CHRIST

About 1647–48. Pen and bistre, corrections in white body-colour; the drawing is cut at the right margin where the head of one of the Holy Maries is still visible. 154×94 mm.
Barnsley Park, Cirencester, Lord Faringdon.

Hitherto unpublished drawing. Rembrandt shows the stone covering the opening of the tomb in form of a cylindrical column keeping faithfully to the text of the Bible: ". . . for the angel of the Lord descended from heaven, and came and rolled back the stone from the door, and sat upon it" (St. Matthew XXVIII, 2).

48. MALE NUDE STANDING, RESTING HIS LEFT ARM ON A CUSHION

About 1646. Pen and wash in bistre. 198×133 mm.
Vienna, Albertina.
HdG 1463; Benesch 709.

About this time Rembrandt, in collaboration with his pupils, devoted careful study to the male human body. As a result of these studies the etchings B. 193, Hind 220, Münz 135 and B. 196, Hind 221, Münz 137 originated. The present drawing apparently served Rembrandt for the preparation of the standing youth in the etching B. 194, Hind 222, Münz 136. The use of reed- and quill-pen combined with brush achieved a rich and picturesque totality. This was in harmony with the increased interest which Rembrandt took in the constructive value of colour.

49. STUDY FOR THE FIGURE OF SUSANNA

Black chalk. 203×164 mm.
Berlin, Kupferstichkabinett.
HdG 46; Benesch 590.

Study for the figure of Susanna in the painting of 1647 in Berlin, *Susanna and the two Elders*, Bredius 516. As a model Rembrandt used here with greatest probability Hendrickje Stoffels, who had entered his household as a domestic help shortly before. Later in life she became the artist's second wife, his support and consolation in the time of his greatest distress. The hard and stony chalk was used by Rembrandt for the development of lines and shades of incredible subtlety.

50. JAN SIX STANDING BY A WINDOW, READING

Black chalk; inscribed by a later hand: Rembrant. 245×191 mm.
Amsterdam, Six Collection.
Benesch 768.

Jan Six, son of one of the most prominent patrician families of Amsterdam was a young man of high intellectual standing, a humanist and writer of Latin poetry. Ties of close friendship connected him with Rembrandt, who etched, drew and painted his portrait on different occasions. The present drawing served as an immediate preparation for the etching of 1647 (B. 285, Hind 228, Münz 70) as is proved by the indention of the outlines with a stylus. It was preceded by a pen drawing, Benesch 767, which represents Jan Six with a greyhound jumping up to his master. Both drawings are still the property of the family of the sitter.

51. THE SACRIFICE OF IPHIGENIA

About 1647. Pen and bistre, with some white body-colour; the upper corners slanted. 248×197 mm.
Paris, A. Normand.
Benesch, Addenda 13.

The humanistic subject-matter may be due to the influence which Jan Six's literary interests had upon Rembrandt. The present drawing is close in style and spirit to the etching *The Marriage of Jason and Creusa* (B. 112, Hind 235, Münz 270) which Rembrandt created as an illustration to a classical tragedy of his friend in 1648. As in the etching the tension of a fateful moment grasps the onlookers who are stricken by horror or turn away in the moment of the terrible sacrifice.

52. THE HOLY FAMILY IN THE CARPENTER'S WORKSHOP

About 1648–49. Pen and bistre. 173 × 227 mm.
Rotterdam, Museum Boymans.
HdG 1347; Benesch 620.

Joseph attends to his carpenter's work while Mary is spinning; to her left the crib or cradle of the Child. The Holy persons are working by lamp-light which pours over St. Mary and outlines St. Joseph as a dark silhouette. The colourful depth of his shadowy figure is suggested by parallel hatches.

53. JAEL AND SISERA

About 1648–9. Pen and bistre, border-line by a later hand. 173 × 254 mm.
Oxford, Ashmolean Museum.
Benesch 622a.

Jael drives a nail into the head of Sisera, who overturns pieces of furniture in his desperate death-struggle. The left arm of Jael was drawn twice, that of Sisera even three times, before Rembrandt decided on the final form. The inclined figure of Jael is echoed by a huge oval mirror pendent above the dramatic scene.

54. THE WESTERN GATE (Westpoort or Utrechtsche Poort) AT RHENEN

About 1647–8. Pen and bistre, wash. 165 × 226 mm.
Haarlem, Teyler Museum.
HdG 1334; Benesch 826.

The present drawing is one of a series of sketches and views of old towns which Rembrandt made on a journey to Eastern Holland as far as Arnhem. The most picturesque and most mediaeval of those sights was the town of Rhenen, which also Hercules Seghers, Ruisdael and other

Dutch artists chose as a motif. The mood of the past was expressed here by Rembrandt in an inimitable way.

55. VIEW OVER THE AMSTEL FROM THE BLAUWBRUG IN AMSTERDAM

About 1648–50. Pen and wash on vellum, arched at the top. 132 × 232 mm.
Amsterdam, Rijksprentenkabinet.
HdG 1208; Benesch 844.

The simplicity and quiet balance of the drawing compared with an earlier example (No. 23) show how Rembrandt increasingly gave up baroque movement and surprising aspects in a motif, replacing them by classical evenness. The effect of luminosity and atmosphere becomes all the brighter.

56. THE SOLDIERS GAMBLING FOR CHRIST'S GARMENT UNDER THE CROSS

About 1650. Reed-pen and bistre. 258 × 188 mm.
Ottawa, National Gallery of Canada.
Colnaghi's Exhibition Catalogue, April–May 1948, No. 48 (S. van Hoogstraten).
Collections: Greville Earl of Warwick (Lugt 2600); J. B. von Ehrenreich (?) "paraphe" (Lugt 2954) in lower left corner; E. Peart (Lugt 892).

The present drawing, listed and exhibited as Samuel van Hoogstraten (Maes has also been proposed), was recently recognized by A. E. Popham as an original by Rembrandt. I acknowledge with gratitude Mr. Popham's consent to have his attribution published here for the first time.
The soldiers play dice for Christ's garment disregarding the death-struggle of the Saviour, Who is seen on the Cross from the back, as a mere accessory and an incidental annotation. The invention is of a grandeur and a human immediacy of which only the genius of Rembrandt was capable. The vain and ridiculous strife of men for worldly gain, not caring for Him, Who is the only one Who matters and Who remains the pivot of all happenings in spite of His neglect which is underlined by the subordinate manner of His representation. The shadowlike figure of a soldier, a mere nothing, is still mocking Him. The vision of this scene is so stirring that it would

have to be attributed to Rembrandt even if the execution did not reveal the characteristics of his hand, as the present drawing does.

Two drawings of the Crucifixion should be compared: Benesch 652 in the Louvre and Benesch 653 in the Bibliothèque Nationale, Paris, Legs Curtis. Mr. Popham draws also attention to the *Stoning of St. Stephen*, Berlin (Benesch 959).

57. SEATED MAN RESTING HIS CHIN ON HIS RIGHT HAND

About 1650–1. Black chalk. 123 × 85 mm.
Stephan von Kuffner Collection, formerly Vienna.
Benesch 1076.

The pose of the man bent forward gave Rembrandt the opportunity of comprising the silhouette into a monumental block which nevertheless is very suggestive of spatial development. A comparison with No. 3 is indicative of Rembrandt's artistic intentions in his late period.

58. OLD MAN SEATED BY A FIREPLACE, WARMING HIS HANDS.

About 1650. Pen and bistre. 149 × 174 mm.
London, P. & D. Colnaghi & Co. (1958).

This hitherto unpublished drawing was brought to my attention by J. Byam Shaw. It is the original of a drawing in Turin (Benesch C 26a). Its style, not clearly recognizable from the copy, reveals it as done at the beginning of the 1650's. Although an every-day subject is represented, the invention comes close to the story of Tobit. Several corrections by the artist in the hands.

59. THE GOOD SAMARITAN ATTENDING TO THE WOUNDED MAN

About 1650. Pen and bistre. 267 × 196 mm.
Barnsley Park, Cirencester, Lord Faringdon.

This hitherto unpublished original was known previously only from an extremely faithful copy at Braunschweig, Herzog-Anton-Ulrich-Museum (Zeichnungen Alter Meister im Landesmuseum zu Braunschweig, Prestel Gesellschaft Pl. 86). Emphasis is laid upon the scenic environment, which may be compared with contemporary landscape compositions.

60. THE HOLY FAMILY

About 1651. Reed-pen and bistre. 153 × 183 mm.
Berlin, Kupferstichkabinett.
Benesch 873.

A quiet idyll showing St. Joseph devoted to his carpenter's work – he is examining a plane – while Mary is fondling her Child. The clear and diaphanous character of the line-work of Rembrandt's late drawings evokes an impression of lightness, even brightness. A luminous atmosphere seems to pervade everything.

61. CHRIST HEALING A LEPER

About 1652. Reed-pen and bistre, wash, rubbed with the finger, white body-colour. 180 × 247 mm.
Berlin, Kupferstichkabinett.
HdG 58; Benesch 900.

The straight strokes of the reed-pen lend a crystalline appearance to the figures. They have a transparent character. Their main traits and features are seized with unfailing certainty whereas accessories fade away in the fluidity of space. The form – so to say – "crystallizes". Rembrandt gives incredible expressiveness to the faces by embedding the eyes in little halos of shadow.

62. THE HOLY FAMILY DEPARTING FOR EGYPT

About 1652. Reed-pen and bistre, slightly washed, white body-colour; the paper has been made up with a strip and a small piece of paper. 193 × 241 mm.
Berlin, Kupferstichkabinett.
HdG 53; Benesch 902.
An old copy is in the British Museum, HdG 880.

The Holy persons are preparing to move from a place of rest. St. Joseph is carefully guiding the steps of Mary to the mule. The forms fluctuate in bright light. It is sunlight which seems to pour over the scene. The brittle and intermitting strokes of the reed-pen combine firmness and exactitude with highest fluidity and mobility.

63. ST. JEROME READING IN AN ITALIAN LANDSCAPE

About 1652. Reed-pen and wash. 250 × 207 mm.

Hamburg, Kunsthalle.

HdG 345; Benesch 886.

This drawing is the preparation in reverse for one of Rembrandt's most beautiful etchings (B. 104, Hind 267, Münz 249), which is famous for its rich scenic setting inspired by Titian and the Venetian masters of his circle. It has little in common with the subtle organization of form which we saw in the preceding drawings – an indication that those are ends in themselves, whereas here Rembrandt intended only to make a layout for his etching. Hence the almost furious impetus of lines and shades which sets the shadowy recess of the Saint in contrast to the majestic climax of the scenery in bright light. Rembrandt did not complete the etching entirely according to this layout but left the foreground unfinished so that the Saint seems to dwell in a circle of sunlight. Rembrandt changed also the incidence of light in the scenery in accordance with this effect.

64. HOMER RECITING VERSES

Reed-pen and bistre; inscribed and dated by the artist: "Rembrandt aen Joannus Sicx. 1652". 255 × 180 mm.

Amsterdam, Six Collection.

HdG 1234; Benesch 913.

The drawing is an entry in the Album Amicorum "Pandora" of the Six family. It is a token of the close friendship which linked Rembrandt with the humanist (see the note to No. 50). Raphael's fresco of *Parnassus* in the Stanza della Segnatura of the Vatican served Rembrandt as an ideal model for the composition, which he transformed into his own language. Rembrandt gave it that quiet penetration and psychical depth which is characteristic of his late style.

65. LION RESTING, TURNED TO L.

About 1651–2. Pen and brush in bistre, on slightly washed paper; inscribed with pencil by a later hand: Rembrandt fect. 138 × 207 mm.

Paris, Louvre, L. Bonnat Bequest.

HdG 751; Benesch 1214.

In his youth, Rembrandt was interested in a variety of animals (see No. 27). In his late period only the majestic lion, the king of beasts, remained. There are sketches of lions done in different years, so that the artist must have had the opportunity of studying them in a Zoo or at travelling shows. He made use of his experience in various drawings and etchings of biblical and religious subjects (see e.g. No. 63).

66. TREES SURROUNDING A GARDEN-DOOR FORMING THE ENTRANCE TO AN ESTATE

About 1652. Pen and washes in bistre; touched with purple-grey Indian ink by another hand. 139 × 198 mm.

Hamburg, Kunsthalle.

Benesch 1285.

The technique of building up trees and forests from layers of parallel hatches was inspired by the study of Venetian drawings and prints (see also No. 75). Rembrandt, nevertheless, achieved the utmost proximity to nature whose breath he seems to have caught in this and similar drawings.

67. LANDSCAPE WITH THE "HUYS MET HET TOORENTJE" (House with the little Tower)

About 1651–2. Pen and bistre, wash. 98 × 218 mm.

Basel, Dr. h.c. Robert von Hirsch.

Benesch 1267.

The motif shows an estate situated on the Amstelveensche Weg, which was one of Rembrandt's favourite excursions outside of Amsterdam. The immense subtlety of the drawing is due to the effect of the technique of dotting, in which Rembrandt followed the model of Pieter Bruegel's landscape drawings. A few washes suffice to suggest the humidity of the atmosphere.

68. VIEW OVER HET IJ WITH SAILING-BOATS AT ANCHOR

About 1652. Black chalk. 103 × 184 mm.

Vienna, Albertina.

HdG 1478; Benesch 1280.

With a few lines of the black chalk Rembrandt knew inimitably how to suggest the recession of the flat country to the hazy depth of the seaside. This and similar drawings formed part of little sketch-books which Rembrandt carried with him on his excursions.

69. FARMSTEAD WITH A HAY-BARN AND WEIRS BESIDE A STREAM

About 1652–3. Pen and bistre, wash, on brownish paper. 120 × 226 mm.
The Hague, F. Lugt.
HdG 776; Benesch 1296.

This farmstead with its impressive grouping of barns and houses attracted Rembrandt's eye so much that he studied it in several drawings from different points of view, near and distant (Benesch 1294, 1295, 1297).

70. WINDMILL ON A BULWARK OF AMSTERDAM (perhaps "Het Blauwhoofd")

About 1654. Reed-pen and bistre, wash. 114 × 202 mm.
The Hague, F. Lugt.
Benesch 1333.

Gun emplacements on the left prove that one of the outposts of Amsterdam's defence is represented here. Even a modest motif like a windmill gains grandeur if set in contrast to the calm and limitless expanse of the Dutch countryside. Windmills formed a favourite subject of Rembrandt's landscape study in painting, etching and drawing. But nowhere did he achieve such monumental and expressive simplicity as in the present drawing.

71. RIVER WITH TREES ON ITS EMBANKMENT AT DUSK

About 1654–5. Pen and bistre. 136 × 187 mm.
Paris, Louvre, L. Bonnat Bequest.
HdG 763; Benesch 1351.

A landscape sketched by Rembrandt with the brush only. The effect even outmatches the works of Claude Lorrain in pictorial dissolution and approaches the art of the Chinese painters. It anticipates the efforts of modern artists from Impressionism to Tachism but far surpasses their achievements. The shadows are translucent and diaphanous in the highest degree.

72. THE TOWER SWIJGHT-UTRECHT AND THE KLOVENIERSDOELEN IN AMSTERDAM

About 1654–5. Reed-pen and bistre, on brownish paper; inscribed by two different later hands: Rembrant; doelen t Amsterdam. 164 × 235 mm.
Amsterdam, A. Boerlage-Koenigs.
Benesch 1334.

Rembrandt omitted the high pointed roof of the round tower for artistic reasons. Even when sketching after nature, he changed the objects according to his compositional intentions.
The building of the Kloveniersdoelen was the seat of the rifle-association which Rembrandt portrayed in his *Night Watch*. It housed the painting until it was transferred to the Rijksmuseum.

73. THE DISMISSAL OF HAGAR

About 1652–3. Pen and bistre. 172 × 224 mm.
Amsterdam, Rijksprentenkabinet, C. Hofstede de Groot Bequest.
HdG 1247; Benesch 916.

The story of Sarah's handmaid is narrated very simply and movingly: her weeping at the farewell, the loving regret of Abraham who has to dismiss her on Sarah's urge and the last blessing which he gives to Ishmael on the threshold of the house. Sarah is observing the scene from the distance unmoved; beside her, little Isaac playing.

74. CHRIST AMONG THE DOCTORS

About 1653–4. Reed-pen and bistre. 188 × 225 mm.
Stockholm, Nationalmuseum.
HdG 1551; Benesch 936.

Characteristic example of that style of Rembrandt's compositional drawings in which he reduced the figures to utmost simplicity so that they take on the shape of articulated dolls. They are, nevertheless, full of spiritual life. The astonishment of the Doctors and their pondering about this miracle are most eloquently expressed. The use of the reed-pen permitted Rembrandt the extreme reduction of his formulae of drawing.

75. THE PROPHET ELIJAH BY THE BROOK CHERITH. I Kings xvii, 3 ff.

About 1654–5. Reed-pen and bistre, wash, some white body-colour. 205 × 233 mm.
Berlin, Kupferstichkabinett.
HdG 81; Benesch 944.

In addition to the drawings with geometrically abbreviated figures (No. 74), Rembrandt drew at the same time others with very monumental figures richer in execution of detail. The quality of crystalline structure is valid for them as well as for the scenery. Compare also No. 76.

76. NATHAN ADMONISHING DAVID. II Samuel xii, 7–14

About 1654–5. Reed-pen and bistre, wash; partly indented for transfer. 146 × 173 mm.
Berlin, Kupferstichkabinett.
HdG 34; Benesch 947.

Rembrandt seems to have planned a painting of this subject because he dealt with the same composition in a drawing in the Metropolitan Museum in New York, Benesch 948. The silent drama of divine blame and rising contrition proceeds between the two men. Rembrandt used for the personification of the Prophet the type of Homer which had deeply impressed him from the time he had made the drawing in the Pandora Album of the Six family, No. 64. It is interesting to note how Rembrandt anticipates in the Prophet and his attitude, which underlines the importance of his words with gestures, the figure of Homer who scans verses to his scribe, a painting which he did almost a decade later for Conte Ruffo in Messina (Bredius 483). The diagonal hatches running over the figures are embedding them into the colourful layers of space.

77. WIDE LANDSCAPE WITH A TREE AND A WINDMILL AMIDST HOUSES BESIDE A CANAL IN THE MIDDLE-DISTANCE

About 1654–5. Reed-pen and wash in bistre. 110 × 242 mm.
Vienna, Albertina.
HdG 1481; Benesch 1356.

The locality seems to be situated on the Amstel River; the path along its bank used to be one of Rembrandt's favourite walks.

78. "HET MOLENTJE", SEEN FROM THE AMSTELDIJK; A BARGE IS BEING TOWED BY A MAN ON HORSEBACK

About 1655. Pen and bistre, wash; drawn on a page of a ruled account-book. 105 × 188 mm.
Oxford, Ashmolean Museum.
HdG 1139; Benesch 1355.

The windmill on the edge of the Amstel River with an inn was a much frequented place of excursion for the Amsterdamers. Rembrandt drew it repeatedly, usually from the opposite bank across the river. The drawing is one of the maturest landscape sketches of Rembrandt drawn with the reed-pen in a style of almost telegraphic abbreviation using intermittent strokes and dots only. Through these abbreviatory signs Rembrandt makes the paper vibrate in a rhythm which is so intense and so close to reality that it almost would not need the support of washes for suggesting the character of time and season.

79. MANOAH'S OFFERING. Judges xiii, 19–20

About 1655. Reed-pen and wash in Indian ink; arched above. 233 × 203 mm.
Stockholm, Nationalmuseum.
HdG 1546; Benesch 975.

Rembrandt, at the end of the 1630's, dealt repeatedly with the subject of Manoah's Offering (Benesch 179, 180), which he conceived then in an entirely baroque way. He seems at that time to have planned a painting which he did not execute, but reflections of this project can be seen in works by pupils like Govaert Flinck and others. In the 1640's, he reworked a pupil's drawing (Benesch 853, Aschaffenburg, Library) in which he first introduced the scenic surroundings with the porched building in the background and a group of the trees at the right. The present drawing and Benesch 974 (formerly Dresden, Kupferstichkabinett), first show the composition in the way in which it is generally known from the painting in Dresden (Bredius 509) bearing the signature: "Rembrandt f. 1641".

F. Saxl put forward the theory (Studies of the Warburg Institute 9, London 1939, fig. 39) that Rembrandt carried out in the 1650's a reworking of the painting as a preparation for which he made the drawing in the O. Reinhart Collection, Winterthur (Benesch 976). It is strange that all drawings which show the composition in the form known from the above-mentioned painting originated in the middle of the 1650's. This brings to our mind that W. Martin with serious reasons doubted the authenticity of the painting in Dresden.

80. NOLI ME TANGERE

About 1655–6. Pen and bistre. 220 × 185 mm.
The Hague, F. Lugt.
Benesch 993.

This drawing combines monumentality of invention with utmost delicacy of presentation. The figures and their setting are suggested by subtle accents and sparing indications so that they seem pervaded and transfigured by the mystery of supernatural light.

81. SELF-PORTRAIT IN STUDIO ATTIRE, FULL-LENGTH

About 1655–6. Pen and bistre, on brownish paper. 203 × 134 mm.
Amsterdam, Rembrandt-Huis.
HdG 994; Benesch 1171.

On the attached strip of paper below, an inscription by C. Ploos van Amstel. Translation: Drawn by Rembrandt van Rijn after himself as he used to be dressed in his studio. Further below, an inscription by Huquier: Rembrant avec l'habit dans lequel il avait accoutumé de peindre.
The drawing offers the most lively idea how the mature Rembrandt looked when at work. It recalls the literary description of Rembrandt given by F. Baldinucci in his Cominciamento, e progresso dell'arte dell' intagliare in rame . . . Firenze 1686, p. 78 ff. on the basis of oral reports of Rembrandt's pupil Bernard Keihl: his square and unpolished appearance, being dressed in old dirty clothes stained with colour because he used to wipe his brushes on them. While working, he would not have received the highest dignitary of the world.

The simplicity and the frugality of the workman devoted to his labour and the inner dignity of a prince in his field are eloquently combined in this vivid sketch.

82. YOUNG WOMAN SEATED IN AN ARM-CHAIR

About 1655–6. Reed-pen and wash in blackish brown bistre. 165 × 144 mm.
London, British Museum.
Benesch 1174.

One of the most magnificent studies of Rembrandt for a portrait proper. The lady wears a Renaissance costume, recalling thus Titian's female models. The vigorous strokes of the reed-pen are supplemented by touches of the brush.

83. SEATED FEMALE NUDE WEARING A MUSHROOM-SHAPED JAPANESE STRAW-HAT

About 1654–6. Reed-pen and olive grey brown bistre, wash with Indian ink. 263 × 200 mm.
London, Victoria and Albert Museum.
HdG 974; Benesch 1123.

In the 1650's, Rembrandt drew numerous studies after the nude female model. They are outstanding in their firm grasp of the plastic form, in their intensive suggestion of the pictorial appearance through powerful strokes of the pen and the brush, and in their keen observation of the play of light on the nude skin. The present drawing is one of the finest examples. The outcome of these studies was not only etchings but also magnificent paintings like the *Bathsheba at her Toilet* in the Louvre (Bredius 521) and the *Woman bathing* in the National Gallery, London (Bredius 437). The Japanese straw-hat which protects this model from intense sunlight was also used as head-dress for Bathsheba's servant in the painting.

84. BOY DRAWING AT A DESK (PROBABLY TITUS)

About 1655–6. Reed-pen, bistre and brush, rubbed with the finger. 182 × 140 mm.
Dresden, Kupferstichkabinett.
HdG 244; Benesch 1095.

The vigorous handling of pen and brush in masterly studies after persons of Rembrandt's entourage reminds one of the broad touch and the radiancy of paint in the contemporary pictures for which the drawings prepared. However, Rembrandt rarely used them as preparatory studies proper. Young Titus drawing or writing was one of his favourite models, and he seems also to be represented here.

85. WOMAN LOOKING OUT OF A WINDOW

About 1655–6. Reed-pen and brush in bistre. 292 × 162 mm.
Paris, Louvre, Edmond de Rothschild Bequest.
HdG 1011; Benesch 1099.

The remarks made in regard to No. 84 apply here with increased emphasis. The interplay of pen and brush creates a fluorescent texture of lights and shades in which the plein-air penetrating through the open window is combined with the half-shadows of the interior to create a total of symphonic richness.

86. A GIRL SLEEPING; STUDY AFTER HENDRICKJE

About 1655–6. Brush and bistre, wash. 245 × 203 mm.
London, British Museum.
HdG 914; Benesch 1103.

The drawing is the result of a momentary impression noted down with fast strokes of the brush and nothing else. Only the mature mastery of a great artist allows of such a concentration and monumental abbreviation without losing a single breath of the pulsating life.

87. INDIAN PRINCE, PROBABLY THE EMPEROR JAHANGIR AS A YOUNG MAN

About 1654–6. Pen and brush in bistre, wash, on Japanese paper. 225 × 170 mm. Copy after an Indian miniature.
Vienna, Albertina.
Benesch 1192.
See the note to No. 88.

The delicate washes with the brush on the silky surface of the paper create a mysterious halo of light around the figure – Rembrandt's way of rendering the hieratic halos around the imperial personalities in the miniatures. In the subtle scale of his monochrome Rembrandt perfectly suggested the spell of colour of the originals.

88. SHAH JAHAN WITH A FALCON, ON HORSEBACK

About 1654–6. Pen and bistre, slightly touched with red chalk wash, on Japanese paper. 219 × 192 mm. Copy after an Indian miniature.
Paris, Louvre, L. Bonnat Bequest.
HdG 744; Benesch 1197.

The universality of Rembrandt's artistic interests is proved by his frequent copies after works of art whose number increased as he matured. They are free translations into his own artistic idiom rather than copies proper, and thus they are works of art in themselves. Works of the Far East met with his deep understanding, as is shown by a magnificent series of drawings after miniatures of the Indian Mogul School. The originals rendered by Rembrandt in these drawings, are to be found in the Castle of Schoenbrunn in Vienna, used as wall decorations in a precious Rococo room. They are of Dutch provenance, although it is uncertain whether they actually once belonged to Rembrandt. The suggestion that Rembrandt drew them as a memento, when he was forced to sell his own collections, is erroneous. The intense study devoted to these works of Eastern art and their inspiring influence can be followed over a period of several years. In spite of all artistic freedom Rembrandt became now more faithful to the originals than he was in his earlier years. It is remarkable that Rembrandt in these drawings approaches very closely the handwriting of the most famous Persian painter, Riza-Abasi.

89. THE CALUMNY OF APELLES. Lucian lix, De Calumnia, 5.

About 1656. Pen and bistre; the paper is enlarged by two perpendicular strips. 263 × 394 mm.
London, British Museum.
HdG 894: Benesch 1207.

Copy after a drawing of Andrea Mantegna in the British Museum (Valentiner 621A), fig. 7.

As in the case of the Indian miniatures, Rembrandt had also reached here a point in his own development which made the drawing by Mantegna particularly valuable to him. He strove to expand the composition in plain relief on the picture surface. He was inspired in his technique of shading with diagonal hatches by Mantegna's engravings and drawings (compare also No. 81). However, what remained tactile surface with the Italian master became with Rembrandt the suggestion of vibrating colour and spatial depth.

90. CHRIST IN THE STORM ON THE SEA OF GALILEE; in the upper right corner, Bust of a frightened Apostle.
About 1654–5. Pen and bistre. 197 × 300 mm.
Dresden, Kupferstichkabinett.
HdG 219; Benesch 954.

Rembrandt had dealt with this subject already in his youth in a painting (Isabella Stewart Gardner Museum, Boston, Bredius 547). In this mature drawing the feeling of swinging movement in a trough of the high-rising sea is expressed much more simply and strikingly. The figures in the boat show the doll-like abbreviation characteristic of the middle fifties.

91. THE HOLY MARIES AT THE SEPULCHRE
About 1656. Pen and bistre, wash; inscribed by a later hand: Rembrant. 159 × 231 mm.
Rotterdam, Museum Boymans.
Benesch 1009.

The feeling of the crypt cut into the depth of the living rock is evoked by the heavy blocklike tectonic forms of the burial place. Even the group of the Maries has the appearance of sculpture framed in stone. The cylindrical block in the lower left corner is the stone which the Maries found rolled away from the tomb according to St. Matthew XXVIII, 2 (see No. 47).

92. THE INCREDULITY OF ST. THOMAS
About 1656. Pen and bistre, corrections with white body-colour. 150 × 240 mm.
Paris, Louvre, L. Bonnat Bequest.
HdG 701; Benesch 1010.

The composition of this drawing shows very clearly how Rembrandt in his late period tried to expand a kind of relief or frieze level with the picture surface. This is particularly emphasized through the step extended like a ribbon in the centre of the drawing. It is the cardinal point around which the figures are balanced in the most subtle asymmetry. Although Rembrandt used the pen only for drawing outlines, he knew how to suggest the radiancy of light emitted by the spiritualized figure of Christ. To His left a zone of blinding light is created in which the figures disappear as in the contemporary etching of 1656, B. 89, Hind 237, Münz 220.

93. FEMALE NUDE WITH HER HEAD BENT FORWARD, ASLEEP
About 1657–8. Pen and brush in bistre, wash, some oxidized white. 135 × 283 mm.
Amsterdam, Rijksprentenkabinet.
HdG 1032; Benesch 1137.

Monumentality of concept distinguishes this female nude which is one of Rembrandt's most powerful creations among his late drawings. Here Rembrandt is up to the level of the great artists of the Italian High Renaissance, whom he surpasses in mastery of colour and light. The surface of the body seems to reflect the light which falls from high up on the recumbent model.
The nude foreshadows the figure of Antiope in the etching of 1659, B. 203, Hind 302, Münz 143.

94. COTTAGES BENEATH HIGH TREES IN BRIGHT SUNLIGHT
About 1657–8. Pen and brush in bistre, wash. 195 × 310 mm.
Berlin, Kupferstichkabinett.
HdG 171; Benesch 1367.

This drawing, which is one of Rembrandt's latest landscapes, excels in grandeur of vision. The groups of trees move in the wind and breathe in bright sunlight. Its rhapsodic character differs from the careful study of nature applied by Rembrandt a few years earlier to similar motifs. It represents an isolated achievement and has only few relatives (Benesch 1364, 1366, 1368).

95. THE RETURN OF THE PRODIGAL SON

About 1658–9. Pen and bistre. 133 ×
199 mm.
Vienna, Albertina.
HdG 1418; Benesch 1037.

This is the latest drawn version of a subject
which, because of its deep human content,
occupied Rembrandt's mind much in his
late period, before he painted the famous
picture in Leningrad, Hermitage, Bredius
598. It is remarkable because of its extreme
simplicity of composition in plain relief
closed in the monumental frame of classicist
architecture. The reunion of father and son
is expressed solely by the quiet harmony of
interlinking curves.

96. THE VISION OF ST. PETER. Acts x, 11–16

About 1658–9. Pen and bistre; at the left,
a strip of paper has been joined to the main
sheet; some pen strokes by an unskilled
hand. 179 × 193 mm.
Munich, Graphische Sammlung.
HdG 396; Benesch 1039.

The Angels lower a large sheet of linen
"knit at the four corners", faithfully illus-
trating the text of the Bible. It is filled with
different animals, among which we recognize a lion, a pig, a camel and the symbolic
unicorn. There, Rembrandt further developed the idea of the etching of Daniel's
Vision of four Beasts, B. 36, Hind 284 D,
Münz 183 D. But the fantasy of Jewish
mysticism is purified into the simplicity and
humanity of the Christian doctrine as we
see in the face of St. Peter – a simple fisher-
man and strong believer who is forced by
divine revelation to overcome his religious
prejudice.

97. CHRIST HEALING A SICK WOMAN
(The Mother-in-Law of St. Peter)

About 1659–60. Pen and bistre, wash, white
body-colour. 172 × 188 mm.
The Hague, F. Lugt.
Benesch 1041.

The drawing belongs to those late creations
of Rembrandt in which the human figure
gains complete predominance. Every action
– e.g. the grip of the Saviour's hands, which

help the woman to rise – is produced with
a striking straightforwardness and simplicity. The spiritual concentration fuses
formal and ethical values to a whole of
almost sculpturesque monumentality.

98. THE ARREST OF CHRIST

About 1659–60. Pen and bistre, wash. 205 ×
298 mm.
Stockholm, Nationalmuseum.
HdG 1556; Benesch 1044.

The strong linear structure with closed outlines symbolizes the petrification caused in
the troop by Christ's magic power. This
power itself becomes visible in the radiant
light emanating from Christ, which is suggested by the clear tone of the paper whereas
the half-tones of washes more or less cover
the surroundings. The woodcuts of the
Small and the Large Passion by Dürer
inspired the group of St. Peter and Malchus.
In the right background the scene of the
fleeing youth is drowned by shadows.

99. ST. MARTIN AND THE BEGGAR

About 1660. Pen and bistre, slightly washed;
inscribed: R. 213 × 152 mm.
Besançon, Musée Communal.
HdG 553; Benesch 1051.

The heavy armour and weapon of the Saint,
an officer in the Roman army, is of that
archaic appearance which recurs frequently
in etchings and paintings of Rembrandt at
the beginning of the 1660's. He knew, as
no other artist, how to evoke the mood of
times of old in order to emphasize the
holiness of the event represented.

100. THE CONSPIRACY OF JULIUS CIVILIS

About 1661. Pen and bistre, wash, some
white body-colour; arched above. 196 ×
180 mm.
Munich, Graphische Sammlung.
HdG 409; Benesch 1061.

Preparatory design for the painting which
may be called the ultimate climax in Rembrandt's activity as a painter. It was ordered
for the decoration of the new City Hall of
Amsterdam, forming part of a series of

paintings on Holland's early history commissioned from different artists. The painting had to fill a large section of the wall in the great hall (ca 6 × 5.5 m.), arched above in the shape of a lunette.

After the painting was placed in 1662 in the position destined for it, the artist had to take it down again for changes requested. It never returned to its place, probably because of the master's reluctance. In order to make use of the painting he cut down the canvas and altered the composition somewhat to the form in which it appears today in this most grandiose document of his late style, fig. 9 (now in the Nationalmuseum, Stockholm, Bredius 482). The drawing, showing some corrections and alterations, was jotted down by Rembrandt on the back of a funeral announcement of Rebecca de Vos, October 25, 1661. Such scraps of paper, and others such as galley proofs, were occasionally used by Rembrandt for sketching in his late years.

101. FEMALE NUDE, WITH A LONG VEIL, SEATED ON A CHAIR BEFORE A CURTAIN

About 1661. Pen and wash in bistre, some red and white chalk. 287 × 193 mm.
Rotterdam, Museum Boymans.
HdG 1033, Benesch 1144.

This and several other drawings are closely connected with the etching of 1661, *The Woman with the Arrow*, B. 202, Hind 303, Münz 144. Compared with the drawings after the nude models from the 1650's (Nos. 83, 93), Rembrandt in his last years abandoned again the clear linear structure which he had most strongly developed in the 1650's and embarked upon a kind of improvising technique using pen and brush in a rhapsodic manner, even inserting some touches in red and black chalk. Thus he was able to visualize the pictorial phenomenon in a most immediate way whose suggestive power far surpasses all his previous achievements of draughtsmanship. The tenderness and mellowness of the nude female body – half plant, half flame – never was expressed so strikingly, although it does not conform with the canon of beauty accepted at the time.

102. THE STANDING SYNDIC

Pen, brush, and bistre, wash, white body-colour. 225 × 175 mm.
Rotterdam, Museum Boymans.
Benesch 1180.

Life Study for the painting of 1662, The Syndics of the Cloth-Makers' Guild ("The Staalmeesters") Bredius 415, Rijksmuseum, Amsterdam, fig. 10.
The Syndic holds in his left hand a pair of gloves instead of the book which he holds in the executed painting. The motif of the gloves was transferred in the painting to the Syndic seated at the far right. The sketching brush seems to indicate at the right a column on high pedestal, a type of scenic device which was common to classicist portrait painting since Van Dyck. The impetuous work of the reed-pen, brush and body-colours creates in the figure an almost terrifying effect of physical and spiritual aliveness, equal to Rembrandt's latest portrait-paintings.

103. ST. PETER AT THE DEATH-BED OF TABITHA

About 1662–5. Pen and bistre. 190 × 273 mm.
Dresden, Kupferstichkabinett.
HdG 229; Benesch 1068.

In this composition ideas come to a close which were first expressed in the paintings *Danae* (1636, Bredius 474) and *Jacob blessing his Grandsons* (1656, Bredius 525). The monumental figures, silent and reverent at the sight of death, are as difficult to decipher in their spatial relations as is the entire setting of the interior. Nevertheless, Rembrandt achieves here an intensity and convincingness of spatial suggestion which surpasses all his earlier achievements. The spectator is drawn irresistibly into the visionary realm of the image, in spite of the fact that the artist emphasized its limits by drawing a frame around it.

104. DIANA AND ACTAEON

About 1662–5. Pen and bistre, wash, white body-colour. 246 × 347 mm.
Dresden, Kupferstichkabinett.
HdG 240; Benesch 1210.

Free transformation of the composition of an engraving by Antonio Tempesta, B. 823, fig. 10. A comparison with the model used by Rembrandt illuminates his power of concentration. Tempesta's engraving shows the figures scattered over a wide scenic stage which impairs the purpose of dramatic narration. Rembrandt assembled them into a tight and close composition in which all main features recur, yet the two opposing protagonists – the goddess and the hunter – are brought into a tense balance. The stage and its devices, however, evaporate and lose all corporeality.

105. THE PRESENTATION IN THE TEMPLE

Signed and dated: Rembrandt f. 1661. Pen and brush in bistre, white body-colour; arched above. 120 × 89 mm.
The Hague, Royal Library.
HdG 1241; Benesch 1057.

Rembrandt created this little drawing as an entry in the Album of a minister of the Dutch church, Dr. Jacobus Heyblock. On the opposite page is a poem of twelve lines relating to the drawing and dated March 30, 1661.

Rembrandt dealt with the subject-matter repeatedly in his late years, and a painting (Bredius 600) which was found incomplete after Rembrandt's death in his studio, was also devoted to it. Apparently the master intended to give in the present drawing the illusion of a little painting closed in its frame. Hence, the pictorial values were stressed foremost and the deployment of a coherent graphic system was abandoned which was quite in line with other drawings of Rembrandt's last years (see Nos. 101, 102). The use of the dry brush, of the pen, of body-colour and of a scraping knife creates a symphonic totality of incredible grandeur – in spite of the smallness of this work of art. Dark and light are elements of the same luminary quality, so that the figures seem to be only condensations of them.

LIST OF TEXT ILLUSTRATIONS

INDEX OF COLLECTIONS